You Were Not Born To Suffer

How to Overcome Fear, Insecurity
and Depression and Love Yourself Back
to Happiness, Confidence and Peace

Blake D Bauer

WATKINS

Sharing Wisdom Since
1893

This edition first published in the UK and USA 2017 by
Watkins, an imprint of Watkins Media Limited
19 Cecil Court
London WC2N 4EZ

enquiries@watkinspublishing.com

Design and typography copyright © Watkins Media Limited 2017

Text copyright © Blake D Bauer 2017

1 3 5 7 9 10 8 6 4 2

Designed and typeset by Clare Thorpe

Printed and bound in Finland

A CIP record for this book is available from the British Library

ISBN: 978-1-78028-985-4

www.watkinspublishing.com

There are two basic motivating forces: fear and love. When we are afraid, we pull back from life. When we are in love, we open to all that life has to offer with passion, excitement, and acceptance. We need to learn to love ourselves first, in all our glory and our imperfections. If we cannot love ourselves, we cannot fully open to our ability to love others or our potential to create. Evolution and all hopes for a better world rest in the fearlessness and openhearted vision of people who embrace life.

John Lennon

To you, the reader

May you be at peace in your heart, healthy, happy
  and free.
And to our world, which is crying out for love, kindness
  and compassion.
May we all learn to love ourselves, each other and all
  life unconditionally.

Contents

Beyond the beliefs of any religion,

There is the truth of the human spirit.

Beyond the power of nations,

There is the power of the human heart.

Beyond the ordinary mind,

The power of wisdom, love, and healing energy is at
work in the universe.

When we can find peace within our hearts,

We contact these universal powers.

This is our only hope.

Tarthang Tulku, Tibetan Buddhist Lama

Preface

This book was first self-published in November of 2012, after a contract with one of the largest personal-development publishers in the world fell through. Following this unexpected shock, in its first edition, *You Were Not Born to Suffer* went on to become the number-one bestselling spiritual title multiple times in Australia, where I was based for over six years. In this new updated edition, you will find very practical insights that have now helped thousands of people around the world to significantly improve their life both personally and professionally. Although legally I cannot prescribe medical advice, I can confidently say that the views and exercises in this book have assisted many people who could not find effective long-term solutions from conventional medicine, psychiatry or religion.

These pages are also a testament to the fact that if you do not let rejection or fear stop you from being true to yourself or from doing what you love, you will find the peace, joy and self-respect that come from honouring your life purpose. In my experience, when we find the courage to value, care for and follow our heart, no matter what, we attract the support we need to live a life defined by truth, kindness and meaning. The external recognition, approval and validation we seek is simply a subconscious cry for us to fully acknowledge our own worth and stop rejecting our true self.

Thankfully I can now always see a larger purpose to my personal struggles. A very significant part of this purpose has been to share the essence of what I've learned from my own suffering with you, so that you can enjoy your life as fully as possible before you die, in the same way I intend to. Our existence is quite fragile, yet we're also much stronger than we realize. And because life is so easy to take for granted as it passes by quickly, it's helpful to know that you're the only person who can give yourself permission to be happy and well. Your partner, spouse, parents, children, employer, doctor or religious leader cannot and most likely will not. Rather, it's a daily choice we each need to make to overcome fear, negativity and guilt.

This book will help you to make this choice.

Believe nothing. No matter where you read it, or who said it, even if I have said it, unless it agrees with your own reason and your own common sense.

Buddha

Introduction

You Were Not Born to Suffer was born out of my personal quest for two things in life. The first was freedom from my own mental, emotional and physical suffering. The second was my unquenchable desire for the truth – the truth about life, the truth about myself and, most importantly, the truth about my life's destined purpose.

Who am I? Why am I here? What is the purpose of life, and of my life in particular? How do I heal myself and find peace mentally, emotionally and physically? Where can I find deep health, happiness and true love? How can I thrive every day rather than just get by and survive? How can I create a fulfilling life that I respect myself for without selling my soul or settling for less than I know is possible?

After finding the answers I was desperately seeking, and helping thousands of people around the world to do the same, the empowering insights I discovered form the foundation for the pages that follow.

I was not aware of it at the time, but as a young man I suffered very deeply in myself, mostly mentally and emotionally, but also physically at times. My early life, like many of our lives, had presented its fair share of painful experiences. Although I could not articulate it until years later, I grew up feeling very insecure and unlovable. I often felt confused, anxious and ashamed of how I felt.

In my attempts to run from both my internal struggles and the challenging situations around me, I unintentionally created a great deal of suffering for myself. On top of the impact of my parents' tumultuous divorce, my biological father's absence, multiple drug-addicted family members, and the extreme psychological dysfunction I was raised around, I developed a number of unhealthy habits through which I caused myself very deep harm. By the time I was 18 years old I had set in motion a domino effect that caused my already unstable world to crumble. I had been suspended from high school on three different occasions. I was selling drugs and had been arrested for drug possession multiple times. I was asked to resign as captain of my high-school football team three games into my senior season after being arrested for driving under the influence of alcohol and several illegal substances. After a night of excessive partying, in the early hours of the morning, I had parked my car and fallen asleep at a stop sign in front of train tracks. Around this same time, I also pushed away my high-school girlfriend while largely under the influence of pharmaceutical pills, which I had no need to take and that had not been prescribed. Even though I loved and cared for her very deeply, I unintentionally hurt her and ruined the relationship through my self-destructive behaviour.

As a teenager I was clearly out of control. I unknowingly used drugs, alcohol and even food as crutches for my broken and confused heart. I had developed a very large and unhealthy ego to survive and to compensate for feeling deeply inadequate and unworthy of love. I wanted so badly to be accepted by my peers, to fit in and be respected, because deep down I did not love myself or feel appreciated at home. As a result, I created a significant amount of pain not only for myself, but also for everyone close to me. I had no idea at this stage that I was running from myself, my life and my past. I didn't know I was denying years of internalized thoughts and emotions, which I had never felt safe to talk about or supported to understand.

Just before graduating from high school, I had cracked my heart wide open and lost the two most important aspects of my life at the time: I lost the girl I loved and both the game (football) and the team I loved. At this point in my development as a person, these two aspects of my life comprised the greater part of my identity, or my ego, and within a very short period I had unintentionally pushed them both away. In retrospect I came to see that through doing this I had lost my sense of self, or who I thought I was. I didn't know this then, but I had experienced what is referred to in psychological and spiritual thought as a 'death of self', where the idea or the image of who we think and believe ourselves to be is completely shattered. I went from being extremely arrogant and thinking I was invincible to feeling painfully insecure, paranoid, self-conscious and tortured by my thoughts, which in reality was always the case underneath the façade I had instinctually created to survive. Although very purposeful in the bigger picture, sabotaging the parts of my life that I loved the most and which offered me an escape from the dysfunction that was normal to me, left me feeling very alone, ashamed and unaware of how to ask for the help I didn't even know I needed.

Reflecting back on it now, as hard as this period was, today I'm very grateful for what I experienced, because it set in motion the birth of my true self as well as the discovery of my life purpose. It showed me how to find the strength, trust and compassion in myself, for myself, that later would prove to be my only refuge or salvation. Without the pain I experienced as a child with my family and the further pain

I created as a teenager, I would not be in a place today where I'm able to look back on this part of my life with a deep understanding of the purpose it served in the unfolding of my destiny. *I now know that I had to lose myself completely in order to heal myself and truly find myself.* Who I had become to survive had to die so that my true nature could flower and guide me towards a life of knowing, loving and respecting myself deeply.

Moving forward after high school, I left home for college still carrying with me my largely unconscious psychological and emotional pain. I went away to college because it was expected of me both by my family and by my local community. Most of the people graduating from the high school I attended were going on to college. I had no real idea of who I was or what I wanted to do with my life at this point. I just unconsciously went with the flow.

I began taking business, finance and advertising classes, because I thought I wanted to make a lot of money, as money seemed to be a very important aspect of life, if not the most. My family and the community I was raised in was very focused on money and material wealth. Growing up I had also witnessed my parents and many family members go through financial hardship or extreme fluctuations in wealth. I watched my mother struggle as a single woman after divorcing my biological father, all of which unknowingly contributed to me developing an excessive drive for financial freedom. As so many of us do, I unconsciously believed that money alone equalled success, strong self-worth and happiness. It wasn't too long, however, before I realized that beyond my physical survival needs, my motives were ultimately empty and meaningless, and that underneath my apparently 'normal' outer life circumstances and goals,

I was completely lost and suffering very deeply in myself. I could see how my fixation on wealth was masking the lack of emotional connection and self-worth I had felt growing up. I didn't know better at the time but I believed that making money would fill the void and heal the pain within me, which obviously would never be the case.

During my second year of studies, after two years of waking up every morning completely tortured by anxious thoughts, I finally found the courage to leave college, step into the unknown, and follow what became an unquenchable desire to heal myself on all levels of my being. Intuitively I knew in my heart that life wasn't meant to be as empty, isolating or painful as I was experiencing it to be. I just knew without doubt that there had to be a way out of my suffering and confusion into a clear and joyful state of being. At the same time, I also held a deep knowing that my life had a purpose and that I would find it if I didn't give up on this quest. Somehow I was certain that I could create a passionate and fulfilling life for myself where I was truly at peace, healthy and happy, engaged in work that was authentic and personally meaningful.

My search for truth, healing and clarity of purpose led me to five universities and to a number of alternative learning institutions. I also continued my studies privately with various spiritual teachers, psychotherapists, herbalists and traditional healers. I formally studied at two different schools for acupuncture and Oriental medicine while simultaneously working with and for a group of Chinese medical doctors. I also visited a number of alternative healers and therapists to help me transform things in myself that I struggled to process on my own. I attended a variety of trainings, lectures, workshops and retreats that focused on holistic healing techniques and spiritual disciplines. I intensively studied and practised various forms of meditation, qi gong, yoga and tai chi on a daily basis for years.

Like many of you reading this book, I became passionately hungry to understand myself and my life. I read book after book on health, spirituality, religion, God, philosophy, psychology, biology, physics, enlightenment, the evolution of consciousness, nutrition and various forms of alternative medicine. All I wanted was to free myself from my mental, emotional and physical suffering and find a clear purpose in my life.

Throughout these years following my decision to leave behind a 'conventional' career and life path, I retreated more and more from the outer world and travelled deeper into the depths of my own being. Like a wounded animal in deep need of healing, I isolated myself from friends and family. I was so desperate for lasting relief that I instinctively did not want to distract myself or numb my mind. Besides going to work, I lived like a monk and focused for hours each day practising the various self-awareness and self-healing practices that I had studied and learned. My search for truth, freedom and clarity of purpose became the focus of all my time and energy.

After roughly six years of concentrating solely on these pursuits, I had thankfully found a depth of clarity and peace within myself. Through studying natural medicine, psychology, alternative healing modalities and spiritual practices so intensively, I learned a great deal about healing myself and creating a healthy, happy and authentic life. Eventually I came to see that everything I had learned in my own selfish quest for wellbeing, purpose and freedom directly transferred over and gave me very practical insights into how I could help others. I found that as I discovered deeper levels of peace, health, joy and passion in myself, I naturally became inspired to support others to find and create the same for themselves. In fact, I felt nothing moved me more than connecting with another human being openheartedly and honestly with a genuine intention to help.

As time progressed I found very deep purpose in supporting others to create a better quality of life. I felt that I had, for the most part, found my life's calling. At the same time however, at the core of my being, I still was not as clear or as motivated each day as I wanted to be. I could feel there was still more to my unfolding destiny that I was not aware of. At some point throughout the suffering and awakening I experienced I became certain that one day I would discover the true reason why I was born and the reason I was on this planet. I knew at this stage I hadn't totally grasped what this was yet, but I also knew that I would indeed find the one thing I was born to wake up every morning for and devote my life to without doubt and without any form of external direction.

I am very grateful to say that the message in this book represents my finally finding what I was looking for.

Towards the end of 2008 I was living in Boulder, Colorado, USA, where I had opened a full-time counselling, coaching and alternative medicine practice. Around this same time, through a number of synchronistic events, I unexpectedly decided to attend a professional training seminar in Australia on a unique form of alternative medicine and kinesiology. Even though I had never been interested in travelling to Australia, I suddenly, out of nowhere, felt a strong urge to fly across the world. I was interested in the techniques being taught and of course in the man who was teaching them, but I strangely felt that the training was not the main reason why I needed to attend.

This unforeseen trip across the world ended up being life changing in so many ways. But the most significant of my experiences there became a major catalyst for this book. I met a beautiful woman at the training who became my best friend and partner for a number of years. I share this because this relationship opened my heart to love in a way words could never do justice in expressing. Having, in the past, hurt both myself and someone I'd loved very deeply – on top of the painful forms of love I'd experienced as a child – I'd unknowingly been scared to love again. I wasn't aware of how much I'd closed myself off to the more vulnerable aspects of true intimacy. This new relationship not only helped me to realize this; it also supported me to open my heart fully in a way I could not have done on my own and that led to the clarity around my life purpose I'd been seeking. The immediate depth, purity and power of the love between us reflected back to me the infinite source of unconditional love within me that I came to realize was my deepest nature. I could see so clearly how it had been covered up by years of stored emotional pain and the limiting thinking I'd adopted to protect myself and survive, all of which was the result of me rejecting my true self.

During the first days of this new relationship, out of nowhere, the following words echoed in my mind as though it was the voice of God. '*Once I love myself unconditionally, loving another becomes an act of self-love.*' Even though I had no clue where they would lead, I grabbed a pen and wrote them down, because the power and significance contained within them impacted me deeply. A few days later, on a plane back to the United States from Australia, I opened the journal in which I had written those words and proceeded to write what became the seed for this book. I had not yet realized that a large part of my purpose in life was to write a book that logically explained how loving ourselves unconditionally and being true to ourselves is the most effective path to optimal mental, emotional and physical health, and then teach this empowering message. I just began writing.

Back in Boulder, Colorado, however, not too long after my return, it became crystal clear to me that throughout my entire educational, healing and spiritual journey, I had simply been learning how to love myself. I could see how all my suffering was caused by me never learning how to relate to myself with kindness, acceptance, respect and honesty at all times. Even in attending five very well-respected universities, studying with highly reputable teachers, and spending hours each day for years deep in meditation, I had simply been looking for love and hadn't understood that I was the love I was seeking. This was when I realized I had to write a book focused on cultivating complete acceptance, kindness and compassion for ourselves as a direct path to healing, happiness and peace. Having suffered so deeply and searched so desperately for this inner knowing and the resulting clarity and freedom I was certain were possible, when it finally surfaced within me, I just knew in my heart, without any doubt whatsoever, that writing this book and sharing this message was what I was born to do.

The insights I began having into loving oneself unconditionally as the key to transforming suffering, depression and disease seemed to be the last piece to this puzzle I had been putting together for years. I could see that in my own restless quest for truth, healing and clarity of purpose I had merely been learning how to value, accept, forgive, honour, trust, believe in, take care of and be true to myself. It became overwhelmingly clear that writing this book would be the most effective way to empower as many people as possible around the world to love, help and heal themselves.

Up until this particular point I'd often felt as though I were stuck in a large and confusing maze that I was always struggling to find a way out of. I knew there was an exit from the frustration and confusion that represented life in this 'maze', but no matter where I went or what I did I could never find complete and lasting freedom. What became crystal clear to me when I finally found the answer I'd been seeking was that it had been within me and present all along. As most of us do, I'd believed this 'thing' I was searching for was outside of myself somewhere in the wider world, when in reality the answers and my true purpose were always within me, just waiting to be discovered and brought forth fully into my life.

Thankfully, I finally grasped the fact that the only way out of this confusing maze that we call life is to go *even deeper into myself*. Although I had heard it before, this was the point where I wholeheartedly realized that *the only way out is the way in*. Like a lock finally clicking into place causing the floodgates to open, I suddenly felt completely aligned with all life, as though the entire universe had come pouring through me, illuminating the path to my lasting freedom. Like a bird that continually flies into a glass window and hurts itself because it doesn't see the glass, I had created a tremendous amount of pain and disappointment for myself because I kept looking externally for something that could only be found in the depths of my own heart and soul. Fortunately, I finally realized that no lasting peace, happiness, fulfilment, worth or self-respect could ever be found in other people or places – and definitely not in the 'things' of the world.

As most of us unconsciously do, I had lived my whole life like a puppy dog chasing its tail. *I was always just looking for love, when in fact I was love itself.* Through not finding what I was seeking externally and coming back to myself over and over again, I realized I organically became what I was looking for. In awakening to this fundamental truth, I realized that the path to finding the source of love within us, which is also the path to embodying the love that we are, is one that requires all of us to answer the evolutionary call to master loving ourselves unconditionally, because this is the only way to truly love others, find peace, be well, or do our personal part to make this world a better place.

With this awareness dominating my consciousness, I sat down to write out my understanding of *how to love oneself practically and effectively*. Having studied the maps and theories extensively, but more importantly walked this terrain myself from suffering and torment into significant liberation and peace, I wanted to outline the most accurate and universal map possible for anyone who truly wants to be healthy, happy and free. I know how hard it can be to articulate with words how deeply you feel, or how much you crave to be lovingly understood and valued. And because I know in my bones how painful, lonely and desperate this quest can feel, I want you to know you are not alone and that there is a solution to your struggles.

Throughout the following pages I have shared everything I've learned from both my own suffering and healing, as well as from my professional success helping thousands of people around the world. This approach has proven effective for many people who could not find practical long-term solutions from conventional medicine, psychiatry or religion. Ultimately, no helping professional can do for you what you must eventually do for yourself in terms of making peace with your life and your past. Someone can witness you, guide you, and be there for you as you process your pain and face your fears, but ultimately no pill or person can 'fix' you.

It will be you who heals yourself and learns how to care for yourself over time.

The heart-centred logic throughout this book will inspire you to overcome your fears so that you can finally free yourself and enjoy your life. If you are willing to take full responsibility and let go of all blame, there is nothing you cannot heal, transform or achieve. In the spirit of living fully before we leave this body and life, this book does not 'beat around the bush'. It is intentionally written to guide you through an inner process that will completely change your life for the better. Between the written text and the exercises throughout, each chapter is designed to create new, healthy neurological and energetic pathways within your mind and body, so that you may begin to direct your thoughts, words and actions towards valuing yourself in every moment and situation. What your life looks and feels like one month, one year, or one decade from now will, however, depend entirely on how deeply you give yourself permission to be happy and well. I love the old saying that goes, 'If you give a man [or woman] a fish he will eat for a day, but if you teach him to fish he will eat for a lifetime.' With this in mind, You Were Not Born to Suffer was created to be a guide on how to effectively fish for yourself so you can find exactly what you want and need.

The tough-love questions now become: what will it take to say you've suffered enough? Where do you draw the line and say enough misery, enough sickness and enough settling? If you're not already dealing with these challenges, do you have to face a life-threatening illness or the destruction of your relationships? If you numb yourself with alcohol, antidepressants, drugs, food, work or material possessions, is this truly what you want for your life? If you have children, or want to have children, is this the example you want to set for them? What will define the moment when you wholeheartedly assert it is time to value yourself and time to stop living a lie? When do you stop pleasing everyone all the time, feeling guilty for your emotions, blaming yourself, apologizing to everyone, or making yourself wrong for wanting to be healthy and happy? When is enough truly enough? And if not now, then when?

I believe we all come into this world *knowing we were not born to suffer*. Although we are very quick to forget, deep in our heart we all know life is meant to be lived and enjoyed with purpose, awareness, respect and kind, meaningful connection. Yes, life will always present us with challenges, but it's how we choose to address them that ultimately determines the quality of our life, health, work and relationships. How we view our mental, emotional and physical struggles therefore leads us either to freedom, happiness and peace, or into more depression, anxiety, loneliness, insecurity and regret.

Thankfully, each moment and day we are given a choice.

Do we remember that we're capable of creating an authentic life that we love? Do we remember that we deserve to be treated with kindness and respect first by ourselves and then by others? Or do we settle for a half-lived life? Do we compromise ourselves and abandon our inner calling? Do we betray our true feelings and constantly allow other people to dishonour, take advantage of and disrespect us?

Looking at this choice objectively, it doesn't seem like much of a choice at all. I would wager my life that every person who reads this would choose the first option and honour it all the time if they knew that everything would work out along the way. Unfortunately, most of us do not value ourselves deeply enough yet to claim the high quality of life that's waiting for every single person. We haven't cultivated a strong enough faith or trust in ourselves, in life, or in the universe to wholeheartedly be ourselves and go after what we want and love. As a result, most of us just settle for less than we're both worthy and capable of, and then we suffer for it. But life doesn't have to be this way.

You can search throughout the entire universe for someone who is more deserving of your love and affection than you are yourself, and that person is not to be found anywhere. You, yourself, as much as anybody in the entire universe, deserve your love and affection.

Buddha

Functional Sanity

As a preface to the rest of this book, it's helpful to know that we are all a bit crazy, in the sense that once we're honest with ourselves we cannot deny the various voices in our head or the countless thoughts that circulate in our mind. I have come to perceive mental and emotional health in terms of practical functional sanity. In other words: *can we take responsibility for our lives in a way that we do not harm ourselves, other people or the Earth while we do our best each day to be well, happy and kind?*

In my experience, which I am sure is similar to your own, there is no such thing as 'normal'. Although it is so common to think 'he or she is normal but I am not' or 'their family is normal' or 'why can't I just be normal?' deep down we all know real life is stranger than fiction. Maybe the reason we can never get to 'normal' is because it does not exist. It's like trying to find a city on a map you're holding, only this city never existed and the person who drew the map did not know what they were talking about. Being normal is mainly about being socially accepted, or, in other words, avoiding the judgement of other people. Of course no one wants to be criticized, but at some stage we have to make a choice between rejecting ourselves in exchange for the approval of others and taking the risk of being honest about our thoughts and feelings, regardless of the consequences.

Eventually you will realize that the pain of rejecting yourself is far greater than the pain of being rejected or judged by other people. So if being normal or socially accepted means you do not speak and act based on what you genuinely think and feel, you will always remain unhappy. This means we're faced with the following questions. *Do you want to be happy or socially accepted? Do you want to find peace and fulfilment or would you rather just fit in? Do you want to enjoy your life, work, physical body and relationships, or would you prefer to be controlled by the opinions, judgements and criticism of others?*

One lesson that helped me tremendously in my quest for happiness, and also strengthened my ability simply to be myself over and above seeking love, approval and acceptance from other people, was understanding the fact that I am not just my thoughts or the voices in my head. Through meditation, self-reflection and healing internalized emotions from the past, I came to know and feel that who I am is far greater than my thinking mind and the conversations I regularly have with myself. Furthermore, I found that most of my confused or contradictory thinking was simply the result of repressed emotions bubbling up as thought. Thinking then became an addiction as well as a means to escape feeling.

When I first realized that I was not happy, I was completely identified with all my thoughts, which were most often connected to feelings of fear, anxiety and insecurity. I believed the dialogue in my mind was 'me' or who I was, because I never learned that who I truly am is more accurately the awareness, consciousness, intelligence and energy behind my thoughts, which surrounds all my thoughts and purposefully gives rise to these thoughts for my own growth, healing and eventual enjoyment of life. Before I realized this, I had no space in my mind or my heart because my body had become cluttered with internalized emotions from the past as well as limiting beliefs I'd inherited from my parents, schooling and society. I now know that without space there can be no happiness, so of course I was unhappy when I was completely attached to my thoughts. Like you,

I had learned to give my power, happiness and sense of self over to my thoughts, thereby allowing myself to become the victim of the conversations in my head, which were most often completely out of control, stress causing and very negative. Thankfully, there is a path to freedom. There is a form of functional sanity that is grounded in a healthy understanding and acceptance of your thoughts.

Self-Love, World Peace and You

I'm sure you've already realized for yourself that most of us never learn how to relate to ourselves with acceptance, kindness and compassion. The majority of us don't even know that it's possible to love ourselves in healthy and conscious ways, let alone what doing so daily would actually entail. There's a growing population of people who know they need to love themselves, but many are at a loss as to *how to do so practically.* In our early years, very few of us had people in our lives who embodied a healthy example of what it means to live and act in the world from a place of unconditional self-love. Today most of us have become so accustomed to the negative voices in our head that we firmly identify with thoughts of criticism, judgement and inadequacy. We're never taught how much freedom or peace is possible beyond this limited and unhealthy way of being.

For generations across the globe, self-love has been judged and shunned as negative and selfish, primarily because very few people actually understand what it means or why it's so important to master. We can't blame anyone for self-love's negative reputation, because most people don't know any better. If they did, they would, first, love themselves unconditionally, and second, always encourage others to do the same. The ultimate truth underneath our collective judgements and resistance to taking care of ourselves wholeheartedly is that we're all merely protecting ourselves from feeling emotional pain. More specifically, we all subconsciously fear what we do not love within ourselves, our lives and our past, because we fear feeling the hurt we ourselves have either created or allowed by relating to ourselves so self-destructively throughout our lives. The unhealthy relationship the majority of us have with ourselves, in our own thoughts, emotions and behaviours, is really the one dynamic that keeps us at war inside ourselves, constantly feeling wounded, angry, powerless, anxious, guilty, ashamed, stressed, unwell or dissatisfied. Deep down we know we have not related to ourselves with the understanding, honesty and respect we desire and deserve, but the implications of shifting this seems overwhelming, so we just deny it or wear a mask each day.

If we do not eventually develop a relationship with ourselves that is based on understanding, acceptance and kindness, it's not only impossible for us to feel good and enjoy our lives, it's also impossible for us to relate to other people in these healthy ways. This is why it's crucial for all of us to understand that our inner relationship with ourselves ultimately determines how we relate to everyone and everything in the world around us. In simple terms, if we judge, reject and criticize ourselves, we will treat others in the same hurtful ways. If our relationship with ourselves remains destructive, then our relationships with other people will remain destructive as well.

The liberating truth that unites all human beings is that we all struggle to love ourselves fully and unconditionally. It doesn't matter how big our ego is, how arrogant we are, how much external success we've had, or how confident we appear. This is the ultimate life lesson that we all struggle with. You, me, the men and women around you right now, wherever you are – your family members, your friends, your neighbours, your colleagues, your boss, your employees, your children, and definitely your parents, and their parents too, all struggle, or have struggled, to relate to themselves with love, kindness and acceptance. It's just the way it's been for generations. But now, we live in a time where more people are waking up and noticing their hunger for a new way of life. We're all ready for new ways of relating to ourselves, to each other and to our world that are grounded in love, kindness and compassion as opposed to aggression. Many people are sick, unhappy, defeated and exhausted from living in such a cold and disconnected world.

Thankfully, learning to love ourselves unconditionally is not only possible, it's also a necessary, natural progression in both the biological and genetic evolution of humanity, and the evolution of human consciousness. This means that life, nature and the entire universe are all working with us and guiding us towards nothing less than total mastery of life's most overlooked and important lesson.

If we do not have love and respect for who we are today, because we both forgive and accept our past and now understand how to value ourselves in every situation, it is impossible for us to truly be at peace. It is not until we make the choice to relate to ourselves with kindness, honesty and respect every day that we finally find the lasting inner peace we crave. So when it comes to our collective destiny as one human family to create peace on this planet, eventually it becomes clear that finding balance and harmony in our own lives is impossible when we relate to ourselves fearfully, aggressively and critically. If we do not live and act from a place of truth and compassion for ourselves, we will just continue to live and act in ways that are not only personally destructive, but that are also damaging for the entire world around us. For this reason, it is crucial to grasp that world peace can only be created by individuals who value inner peace, compassionate understanding, mutual respect and loving-kindness above all else. If we aggressively try to change the world or other people, without honestly transforming our own anger, hurt, judgement or habits of denial, no amount of effort, force or war will bring about the lasting changes our world needs.

There is no difficulty that enough love will not conquer.
There is no disease that enough love will not heal.
No door that enough love will not open. No gulf that
enough love will not bridge. No wall that enough love
will not throw down. And no sin that enough love
will not redeem. It makes no difference how deeply
seated may be the trouble. How hopeless the outlook.
How muddled the tangle. How great the mistake.
A sufficient realization of love will dissolve it all.
And if you could love enough you would be the
happiest and most powerful person in the world.

Emmet Fox

Using the Word *God*

Using the word *God* can be a very sensitive subject. It is a word that holds the power to create either separation and war, or unity and peace. For this reason, I feel it's important to clarify and define the meaning of the word *God* as it is used throughout this book. I chose to use the word God in some places because it very effectively brings to the surface our feelings and beliefs about life, truth and love.

As you read, please keep in mind that I respect each religious tradition and spiritual path. In my own life, I have found that (1) all religious and spiritual study eventually leads to love and kindness in various forms, and (2) the only barriers between one human being and another are the unhealed emotions in our hearts and the limiting beliefs we hold in our heads. These two realizations have shaped and inspired much of this book.

In using the term *God*, I am referring to everything and everyone in the universe, including the space in which no physical forms of life and no physical objects exist. By this definition, God refers to the intelligence, awareness, source, love and atomic energy from which all life and all physical forms of matter in the universe arise. From this perspective, God exists in all people, all things and all space, as the people, things and space themselves. God, here, also represents the vast sea of unlimited potential, possibility and energy to which all life and all physical forms of matter eventually return.

Essentially my view is that there is nothing and no one that is not God. Every event, every circumstance, every tear, every joy, every form of life and every painful lesson is God. In the spirit of being practical, however, in my experience God is seen most clearly through unconditional love, kindness, acceptance, respect, understanding and forgiveness, both for ourselves and for other people. Paradoxically, God is also always in our pain, heartbreak, depression, illness, loneliness and relationship problems, which is harder to see. Although words are merely words, and will always fall short of the actual truth towards which they point, the word God here ultimately refers to the love that is crying out through our struggles to be expressed more fully in our body, mind, life, daily work and world.

I have found the paradox, that if you love until it hurts, there can be no more hurt, only more love.

Mother Teresa

CHAPTER 1

The Butterfly

The Greek name for a butterfly is Psyche, and the
same word means the soul. There is no illustration
of the immortality of the soul so striking and beautiful
as the butterfly, bursting on brilliant wings from the
tomb in which it has lain, after a dull, grovelling,
caterpillar existence, to flutter in the blaze of day and
feed on the most fragrant and delicate productions
of spring. Psyche, then, is the human soul, which is
purified by sufferings and misfortunes, and is thus
prepared for the enjoyment of true and pure happiness.

Bulfinch's Mythology: The Age of Fable

The life cycle of a butterfly is a perfect example found in nature that mirrors back to us what it means to break free from the limitations and fears that stop us from living our most authentic, liberated and joyful life. The caterpillar's metamorphosis into a butterfly demonstrates the natural processes of inner and outer transformation that we all experience. In its physical form, the butterfly symbolizes the potential freedom and light-heartedness that are available to each and every one of us. This is why just seeing a butterfly reawakens us to the magic and wonder inherent in life. Its grace and vulnerability immediately take us beyond thought into the mystery of our own existence.

The butterfly begins its journey as a caterpillar, and it may or may not be aware of what it is destined to become. But the caterpillar lives on, faithfully following the inner prompts arising within its being. It *feels* its way through life, naturally following the inner direction with which it was born. The caterpillar follows what seems to be an inner plan, which from the outside can be observed as guiding the journey from caterpillar to cocoon and from cocoon to butterfly. The feeling and the pull into what appears to be the unknown must be so clear and so strong for the caterpillar, because when the time comes to create a cocoon for itself, the caterpillar carries out its intended purpose with a one-pointed focus and determination.

The caterpillar appears to feel that it does not have a choice, but that it must surrender and follow the forces of nature and the universe as they propel and guide it forward, no matter what the journey entails. Once transformation is complete, the butterfly struggles with all of its strength to emerge from its cocoon. Eventually it leaves behind the protective shell that no longer serves any purpose.

The butterfly's new existence only slightly resembles its old form. It does not know itself any more. Its past has been left behind, and the butterfly now experiences itself as something changed and new. It has been reborn. And now it is free.

Our own journey through life is like this as well. Like the caterpillar's journey into its cocoon and its struggle to emerge as a butterfly, our own journey as human beings towards our most liberated and joyful life is one in which we also struggle to live gracefully and intentionally as a free and full expression of who we truly are. We all struggle to liberate ourselves from our suffering and thus free ourselves from our protective cocoon in order to embody the highest form of our own evolution and potential. Within each of us, there lives a sense of an inner plan that is always inspiring us to break free into the mystery of our existence. We too have this inner guidance directing us forward, a felt force deep within our soul propelling us onwards in faith. Just like the butterfly that struggles to break free from the restricting confines of its cocoon, somewhere deep down we somehow know and trust that our own struggles will eventually open to the richness, wonder and beauty of our most liberated and joyful life.

Ultimately, the struggle to free ourselves fully is the struggle to relate to ourselves with loving-kindness, honesty and respect in every moment and situation. To do this we're all called to heal our internalized psychological and emotional pain in the present. We're faced with the task of releasing ourselves from the protective cocoon that we've developed over time – the psychic shell that's been protecting us until we were ready to live our lives authentically and openheartedly as a full expression of our true self.

Just as with the butterfly, the development of our own cocoon is natural and vital for our soul's evolutionary unfolding. Our cocoon serves us while we heal and go through the inner transformations necessary to be and accept ourselves fully. At some point, however, our cocoon always becomes limiting and unhealthy. Once we've gone through the initial stages of growth within the safety of this protective shell, all of us are called to liberate ourselves from a limited way of being in the world that no longer serves us. When this time comes will vary for each of us, just as buds on the same branch open at different moments, but it does indeed come. And when it does we're all faced with a life-defining choice. We either surrender and align with the forces of nature and the universe that are evolving within us, or we resist this evolutionary force, remain in denial, and thereby invite more struggle and pain.

A moving story I once read demonstrates this perfectly. It tells of a woman who brought two butterfly cocoons into her home that were about to hatch. The woman wanted to observe the butterflies break free from their cocoons. So for days she eagerly watched, waiting for the butterflies to emerge. In time, she was able to witness one butterfly begin creating a small hole, and from the woman's perspective, this first butterfly seemed to struggle painfully as it slowly pushed its way through the opening it had created. Once liberated, the butterfly lay there on the table, exhausted and unable to go any further. However, after a short period of time, it finally raised itself up and flew out of a nearby window, fluttering on its strong and beautiful wings.

After observing the challenging process that the first butterfly experienced, the woman felt inspired to help the second butterfly free itself from its cocoon so that it wouldn't have to struggle as the first one did. Meaning well, the woman decided to use a razor blade to slice gently down the centre of the second butterfly's cocoon. Once free, the second butterfly lay there on the table just as the first one had. However, after a similarly short time, rather than raising itself up and flying away, the second butterfly quietly died. Confused about what had occurred, the woman contacted a friend who was a biologist and asked her to explain why the second butterfly had died. Her friend explained that the struggle the butterfly undergoes to liberate itself from its cocoon actually forces liquids from deep inside its body cavity out into the tiny capillaries in the butterfly's wings. The process of pushing its wings up against the inner walls of the cocoon is what causes them to harden, making them strong enough for their new life of flight. Without the struggle a butterfly experiences in breaking through its cocoon, there could be no strength in its wings, no flight, and ultimately no life.

Like the butterflies in this story, you and I are destined to free ourselves from our own protective cocoon. Our ego, our fears and the limiting beliefs that keep us stuck simply protect us from the pain, discomfort and truth we'd prefer to avoid. But just like the caterpillar, we each have everything we need within ourselves to be free. When we stop to reflect on the deeper meaning of this story we are graced with one of life's most beautiful and empowering lessons: *we already have everything we need within our self to fulfil our life's purpose and realize our greatest potential. We are not lacking in any way. The intelligent universe, or God, created life inherently to possess all that it needs within itself to fully become what it is destined to be.*

Unfortunately, too many of us live our whole lives without realizing this. We're not taught to trust ourselves, but rather we learn to listen to other people and to doubt our inner wisdom, which leads us to prefer the familiarity and safety of our cocoon instead of truly living. We unintentionally end up settling for a limited way of life, typically lying to ourselves in some way and having never realized or expressed the fullness or the greatness of who we truly are. If we don't just settle for cold comfort, most of us constantly search outside of ourselves, thinking that something or someone beyond us will free us. Maybe someone will heal, rescue or save us? Maybe someone will love us enough or care enough to liberate us from our personal struggles and make everything okay?

Like you, I have learned the hard way what an illusion this truly is.

Each person is born a caterpillar and we all create a cocoon for ourselves as we grow. What differs among us, however, is that some of us are willing to follow the inner prompts of our heart and soul to become the liberated, passionate and purposeful being that we're destined to be, and some of us quite simply are not. There seem to be only two options in life. Either we become the butterfly we're destined to be, or we don't. Either we master loving ourselves unconditionally, and in so doing free ourselves from our cocoon, or we don't.

In the first option we undoubtedly struggle; sometimes we struggle deeply and it's painful. But with the struggle and the pain always come the beauty, peace and magic of living our most liberated and joyful life. The struggle and pain actually become worth it because we finally respect ourselves for the courage and strength we found to live an authentic life. We get to experience the powerful loving truth and natural intelligence that are inherent to our deepest nature. In essence, we get to be free, and one could say that our soul gets to fly.

In the second option, we either settle for the fear-based comfort of our cocoon or we wait for someone or something to come along and free us. We might live our whole lives waiting for someone to slice open our cocoon for us. In both cases, we end up living unaware that we already have everything we need within us to liberate ourselves and live an authentic meaningful life both personally and professionally. When we take this second path we remain deeply frustrated and unsatisfied, and nothing and no one is ever enough for us because ultimately we're not taking responsibility for what only we can and must do. Eventually our bodies stop functioning before we ever give ourselves permission to be truly happy. We leave this world and lifetime with regret, having passed up the magic, wonder and beauty that's here now waiting for all of us to claim.

I personally feel that a life without having learned to love myself unconditionally would not have been worth living. In fact, I don't know if I would be alive today had I not found the deep compassion and understanding for myself necessary to truly value and be myself. If you're honest in reading this, I'm sure you'd agree that the suffering and confusion that result from a critical, insecure, fear-based or self-destructive relationship with yourself make life quite miserable and hardly worth living at times. Feeling misunderstood, alone and disconnected is no way to live, but we have to learn to matter to ourselves mentally, emotionally and physically before this can shift and before we can simply feel good in our body.

CHAPTER 2

The Purpose of Suffering, Depression and Disease

The world breaks everyone, and afterward, many are strong at the broken places.

Ernest Hemingway

Wherever you are, please take a few slow, deep breaths into your belly. Feel your whole body, from your feet all the way up to the crown of your head, and then down to your fingertips. Please relax any tension you feel and let yourself be. Using each inhalation to open your body and create inner space, welcome everything you're thinking, feeling and experiencing here in this moment. Please be present to your body and your breath.

Everything happens for a reason, especially health challenges of the mind and body. Although this may be difficult to accept, I've found that many of us unintentionally allow ourselves to get depressed or physically unwell, because we never learned how to express our emotions or care for ourselves in the ways necessary to remain healthy and happy throughout life. We learn from a young age to please others and to seek our parents' or our caregivers' conditional love to survive, but it's often at the expense of being true to ourselves and it causes us very deep harm. If we never wake up to this unhealthy internal dynamic, it eventually leads to depression, disease, relationship problems and most forms of suffering, all of which are simply cries from our soul calling us back home to ourselves, to the source of peace and strength within, and ultimately to love and value ourselves in each moment – starting now.

Early in life we learn to feel scared, guilty and ashamed to some degree about expressing what we feel, need and want, because this was apparently too selfish or burdensome for the people around us. Although everyone is actually selfish, but most often in denial about this, today many of us have become accustomed to living in fear. So now, after years of pleasing others and not looking after ourselves, we often find ourselves unhappy, unwell, or full of resentment, anger and regret.

Confused, we ask ourselves: *How did I get here?*

No one is a bad person for wanting to live a deeply fulfilling and authentic life. You are not a bad person for wanting to be healthy, happy, understood or fully met within a loving relationship. Yet we still feel shame for having these desires. We've unintentionally become entrapped in a web of our own weaving, because we have not realized that we're waiting for a wholehearted commitment to our own wellbeing and that our suffering is simply asking us to speak and act based on what we truly feel in each situation.

I cannot help but point out the fact that modern conventional medicine has not discovered cures for ailments like cancer, autoimmune disease and clinical depression. Is it because there's no cure? Or is it really because we've been viewing these illnesses and symptoms from a limited perspective and completely missing the purpose of these challenges? Could it be that we've been looking for the root causes in the wrong places?

I believe so.

Based on my experience working intimately with tens of thousands of real human beings, I've found that our mental and emotional health is both the cause of and the solution to most forms of personal suffering. Our ability to express what we feel effectively, overcome negative thinking and act in alignment with our true emotions, needs and desires, directly determines the quality of our overall wellbeing. Just because we cannot see something does not mean it's not real. Just because we don't directly watch the destructive process of non-physical toxicity developing into physical toxicity doesn't mean it's not accurate or valid. If I said that the genuine love you feel for your partner, spouse, child, parent or pet was not real, how would you respond? I think that makes this point clear.

I've discovered that in most cases deep unhappiness and chronic illness are the result of the self-destructive, critical, judgemental and fear-based relationship many of us developed towards ourselves in childhood, which then leads to a weakened immune system, increased susceptibility to viruses, bacteria and environmental toxins, and ultimately to a lack of healthy self-care. Because we tend to be so lost in this harmful way of thinking and acting, since it's all we've ever known, it's very easy to overlook the apparently naïve possibility that transforming our mental and emotional dis-ease can bring the long-term relief and peace we're seeking.

Life seems to take away anything or anyone we take for granted. Our life itself and our health fall into this category also. I have witnessed time and again how individuals ignore and disregard their mental and emotional life, simply because they don't know how to honour it or talk about it effectively. Rather, we've all learned to use denial to survive, and the natural progression of this sentiment is a deep feeling of worthlessness, where one perceives that one's feelings, needs and desires do not matter. We often feel our inner self or soul has no value or is not appreciated by the people around us, and the by-product of this is a body that does not seem to matter or feel worthy of attention either. Basically, a heart not cared for or respected by ourselves becomes a body that does not feel good to inhabit. And this becomes a very vicious cycle that a person can actually get used to and allow to ruin their life.

To be frank: what's the point of being alive if our soul feels trapped, misunderstood and valueless? What sentient being would ever want to continue to live a mentally tortured, emotionally anxious and overwhelmingly stressful life? Yet we as human beings feel unworthy of creating a lifestyle, career and relationships that make us feel good, alive and well on a daily basis. Although objectively it seems natural to desire a healthy and happy life, we are persistently held back by the guilt, fear, shame and underlying hurt inside us. We live feeling disconnected, while this internal toxicity trickles down inside like acid or parasites slowly eating us alive. Addiction and suicide can be understood in this light, especially when we recall what it's like to feel we do not matter, silently suffering alone, without any idea of where to find love, understanding or healthy long-term relief.

The body's suffering is a mask the mind holds up to hide what really suffers.

A Course in Miracles

As a culture and as individuals we need to swing the pendulum of attention towards transforming our dysfunctional mental and emotional life if we want our body and outer world to reflect a healthy internal environment. But before we can take these steps we have to find the humility to open our mind, especially if our current approach is not getting us the results we want. We have to admit that we didn't know better and acknowledge that maybe our views have been limiting or not very healthy for us. This is not about making ourselves wrong, thinking we are flawed or blaming ourselves. Rather it's about recognizing the fact that we inherited some very self-destructive habits and beliefs from people who were doing their best, with what they knew, at the time. And now, our body, life and world is screaming out for us to finally heal our heart and mind.

For me, traditional Chinese medicine offers one of the most practical and logical insights into how our thoughts and emotions can lead either to health and happiness or to depression and disease. From this worldview the causes of physical and mental illness directly correlate to the flow of energy and blood in the body. In simple terms, when energy and blood are free-flowing daily we experience health, happiness and freedom from pain. But when they stagnate we will eventually encounter tiredness, depression, physical pain, weakened immunity and the toxic build-ups that cause serious disease.

This perspective asserts that blood in the body follows the flow of life-force energy. The best example of this is the energetic beat or pulse of the heart that causes blood to flow within our veins and carries our immune cells, hormones, vitamins, minerals and other nutrients to all corners of the body. What is often overlooked in Western conventional medicine is the link between internalized thoughts and emotions that, coupled with fear and the resulting inaction, lead to a decrease first in the healthy flow of energy and blood, and then logically to the impaired function of the various systems throughout the body, such as the nervous, circulatory and digestive systems.

Consider for a moment that a 40-year-old person, who has on average been awake for 16 hours every day and thus slept for 8 hours each night, has been alive and awake for 840,960,000 moments or seconds. That's 14,016,000 minutes of life experience in which this person has been feeling and thinking something directly connected to their deeper wounds, needs and desires. Objectively, much of this inner process is made up of unresolved emotions and confused thoughts, which constantly circle the mind and body and are rarely expressed or addressed in a way we're at peace with. This unhealthy internal environment typically leads to unhealthy lifestyle choices or addictions, which only cause more health problems, weakened immunity and life challenges.

Both thought and emotion are subtle forms of atomic energy, which when repressed constantly over time cause internal stress, limited oxygen intake and imbalances in molecular and cellular processes. Such repression also causes the flow of life-force energy and blood to slow down and become severely blocked. Due primarily to the various manifestations of fear, insecurity and people-pleasing habits, most people don't act based on instinct, intuition, self-care and what their heart truly communicates, which creates further disruptions to the healthy flow of energy and blood in the organs and circulatory system. Symptoms like anxiety, shallow breathing, chronic fatigue, lethargy, digestive disorders, depression, bipolar disorder and insomnia set in, and we, and often our doctors, are not quite sure what the underlying cause is.

Eventually, over days, weeks, months and years of this process guiding both our life and our behaviour, the blood and fluid in our bodies begin to coagulate to such a degree that nodules, masses, growths and tumours start to form. This then leads to toxins building up in the bloodstream, fat tissue, muscles and organs, resulting in chronic pain and disease. In simple terms, our body becomes at war with itself on a cellular level because we are at war with ourselves mentally and emotionally. The miraculous intelligence of the body produces physical symptoms to alert us to the tear between what we really feel, want and need, and the fears that stop us from taking good care of ourselves, speaking honestly and following our heart. Although we're not aware of it, living a lie and constantly rejecting our true self is exhausting and eventually breaks us down physically and mentally.

From this viewpoint it's easy to see how living a stressful life compounded by work that is unfulfilling, or staying in relationships where we are not true to our deeper emotions, can create significant internal pressure on our major organs and central nervous system. If we are constantly fighting ourselves in this way, and do not listen to the messages from our body, the inevitable result is our self-destruction. This does not account for excessive consumption of alcohol, food or drugs, whether recreational or prescription, which are habits motivated by a desire to numb deeper mental and emotional pain. Often this is a misguided quest for short-term relief that only makes our health concerns worse in the long run. These crutches for our broken heart mask our feelings of not being worthy of love and the burden of living in perpetual fear.

My view is that both genetic and acquired immune system problems all stem from this dynamic. If we are destructive in our thoughts, emotional life, behaviour and lifestyle habits, over time the decrease in blood and energy flow, as well as the build-up of toxins, lead to a weakened capacity to fight off infections from bacteria, parasites and viruses. Similarly, a toxic or parasitic mental and emotional life leads us to allow toxic and parasitic people to remain in our lives, which directly correlates to an increased susceptibility to all forms of pathogens and environmental toxins that will further eat away at our health, happiness and peace when we allow it.

Most people understand that eating natural whole foods and adopting a healthy lifestyle will support wellbeing and prevent illness. What most don't know, though, is that complete honesty, vulnerability and love for oneself in every situation is just as vital to our long-term mental and physical health. We are so used to hiding our true feelings in order to survive, keep the peace and protect ourselves from judgement, criticism, aggression and rejection that we remain unaware we're relating to ourselves in such a harmful way, or allowing others to take advantage of us, until of course we are forced to figure out why we've become so depressed or ill.

Deep down we all know there has to be more to life than suffering. But no one can save, heal or free us besides ourselves. This is precisely why the purpose of mental, emotional and physical symptoms is to show us where and how we're not caring for ourselves well enough to thrive and flourish fully before we die. Once we understand the simple but profound truth that all suffering is the result of a constant rejection of the true self – a self that we never learned how to love, accept, value and care for properly – we can begin transforming whatever struggles we're faced with and find deeper peace and health immediately.

Depression and disease is our body's practical and logical way of alerting us to the life-or-death importance of giving ourselves permission to be fully who we are now. I have witnessed countless people stop being victims to their fearful and insecure thoughts, which empowered them to transform their suffering into a better quality of life. Once they wholeheartedly committed to speaking and acting in a way that valued their deeper feelings, needs and life purpose in every situation as the priority, even when scared, they were able to heal and forgive their past, and finally stop hurting and betraying themselves in the present.

The key, then, to the breakthrough is to stop running from yourself. Most of us today are moving through life so fast that we're lost in a momentum of distraction, going from one person or place to the next, without ever slowing down. But if you can choose to create some space to be alone and stay open to yourself you can finally welcome your inner truths and *feel* deeply again. Then you can get clear about what you actually want in life, what feels good to you, and what makes you feel alive and well. I've found that when we focus primarily on these things daily, even when criticized for doing so, we support the healthy flow of energy, blood and emotion in the body and we naturally move away from any person, situation or habit that is no longer healthy for us.

Until we open our mind to our inherent capacity to heal ourselves and thus take our life, health and happiness back into our own hands, there will always remain aspects of ourselves that are closed and thus will not heal. It doesn't matter how many doctors we visit or how great a practitioner might be. The walls of the ego and the small separate self must come down, which can only happen through bringing our own loving attention and acceptance to all the parts of us we've rejected and hidden over the years. Regardless of how hard life has been to date, I've found that it's only through taking one hundred per cent responsibility for the depression, disease and worldly struggles we're experiencing that we can finally see the purpose this suffering has served in bringing us home to our true self and to the source of strength and peace within. Blaming anyone or anything external only wastes the time and energy we need to heal and free ourselves now. If we choose pride or stubbornness over honest vulnerability, our denial will only keep us trapped.

> *No one decides against his happiness, but he may do so if he does not see he does.*
>
> *A Course in Miracles*

The moral of this story is that even when we cannot see it, and even if we won't allow ourselves to believe it, there is a much healthier and happier way of life waiting for all of us beyond the aspects of our lives with which we're currently struggling. I've found that the single most important key to finding lasting peace is the realization that all suffering is simply a cry from our body and subconscious asking us to love, accept and value ourselves now. All the mental, emotional, physical, financial and spiritual struggle we experience is purely our soul's way of waking us up to the aspects of ourselves, our lives and our past that we haven't yet learned how to love or understand fully.

Depression, disease, insecurity and pain force us to bring more awareness into our daily lives so we realize the value of living with kindness and compassion for ourselves, other people and all life. Our suffering actually stops us from running and reawakens us to the truth in the present, so we can transform whatever does not support our wellbeing or life purpose. Our struggles are meant to help us learn the lessons beneath what we perceive to be our 'mistakes', so we can live each day in a way that creates less suffering and more harmony, not only for ourselves, but also for everyone around us.

Suffering is irrefutably a part of life. It always has been and to some degree it probably always will be. But the amount we suffer and the excess pain we create can be significantly decreased and relieved once we understand how we bring it upon ourselves. The pain of not loving ourselves is how we learn to value ourselves sooner rather than later so we can enjoy the life we've been given.

It's empowering to know that anxiety, confusion, sadness, frustration, anger, hurt, resentment, fear, shame, guilt, regret, insecurity, inadequacy and self-doubt are all merely the result of us not knowing how to love and value ourselves in the past. All the pain we've ever felt, feel now or will ever feel has its roots in the moments where we have not been true to ourselves, but rather have compromised, betrayed, abandoned, judged, rejected and therefore hurt ourselves. When we accept this universal truth and apply it to our life we can finally free ourselves from all the additional suffering we unintentionally allow. I'm sure you agree that life is challenging enough without us being our own worst enemy.

There is no coming to consciousness without pain.
People will do anything, no matter how absurd,
in order to avoid facing their own soul. One does not
become enlightened by imagining figures of light,
but by making the darkness conscious.

Carl Jung

The only way to move beyond our identification with our struggles is to view these apparent obstacles as lessons to be learned that are making us stronger and better people. Regardless of how much we try to avoid pain, if we run from it or numb ourselves it will remain alive inside us, not only making us sick or miserable over time, but also causing us to react to life in ways that sabotage our relationships, goals and dreams. A large number of us live our whole lives trapped in some form of suffering because we keep denying the specific truths that seem too overwhelming, unlovable or scary to address. We never learned that through stepping into the unknown and honestly talking about these inner battles we can transform them, grow from them and ultimately thrive because of them.

Each thought, emotion and life experience can guide us towards improved health, happiness and self-respect if we can stop fighting life and find the purpose in what's challenging us. Every single situation and relationship – past, present and future – is leading us towards an unconditional love for ourselves and the freedom that we know is possible. In fact, the more we value ourselves, the clearer it becomes that our suffering in all its manifestations exists to guide us directly towards joy, kindness and truth. It creates the fork in the road we need to make choices to open rather than contract, to surrender rather than hold on to what's not healthy for us, and to care for ourselves rather than live in guilt, denial or fear.

Practical Questions

At the end of most chapters in this book you will find questions specifically designed to transform the core psychological and emotional blocks that are holding you back in life. These questions will assist you in freeing emotion and energy that are trapped in your body and life so you may release whatever is hindering your peace, health and happiness. As you work through these self-healing questions, it will be tremendously helpful to write out your answers, because expressing your thoughts and feelings in this way will help you to honour and clarify what is true for you. It will also free the psychological, emotional, physical and spiritual energies that have become stuck. For this reason, I highly recommend that you purchase a journal or notebook in which to write your answers. The potential change and forward movement these questions can inspire is truly unlimited.

Key Affirmations

Following the questions, you will also find affirmations at the end of most chapters in this book. These practices will support you to think, feel and express positive, healthy and high-vibrational thoughts and words. As I mentioned before, the confronting questions will free vital life-force energies that have become trapped in your body, heart, mind and life. Once liberated, these energies are then available for you to channel or redirect towards thinking, feeling, speaking and acting in ways that support you to create what you want and need. With this in mind, I have found that working with the affirmations directly after answering the confronting questions that precede them is a very effective way to transform the limiting beliefs and unhealthy thought patterns that are harming you. Additionally, I highly recommend using the practice outlined in the section opposite for all of the affirmations contained in this book. *To make doing this simple, I recommend marking the next page so you can refer back to it after reading each chapter.*

Lastly, it's important to know that affirmations are not effective in many cases if you're not also speaking and acting based on what you truly feel in each life situation. This is why if you look in the mirror and try saying 'I love you' to yourself, but you are currently betraying yourself in your life, your initial reaction will be disbelief in the affirmation and criticism of yourself, because the truth is you're treating yourself horribly rather than with love or respect. Once you begin to address the areas where you're not valuing yourself, you'll know in your heart that you're taking care of yourself and the affirmations then become a very powerful support to improve your life.

Additional Ways of Working with Affirmations

With your eyes either open or closed, wherever you are, please say each affirmation one at a time. If you are alone and you would like to say them out loud, please do so. If you are around other people and feel more comfortable expressing them only to yourself, that is very effective too. Either way, please feel your whole body as you express each affirmation. Please feel your feet, your legs, your belly, your chest, your back, your arms, your hands, your neck and your head. Take a few slow, deep breaths through your nose into your belly, and then imagine that you are speaking to every cell in your body. When you have an opportunity, please also try expressing these affirmations in front of a mirror while looking into your eyes. This is a very powerful way to help yourself.

Please also note any negative thoughts, emotions or physical sensations that arise within you as reactions to the affirmations you express. These will represent your subconscious blocks to living a fully healthy and happy life. Once aware of these inner limitations, you'll be empowered to love yourself more deeply and reaffirm the positive, healthy thought patterns necessary to harmonize the negative energies that are trapped in your mind and body.

Finally, please consider that it takes a little time to create new, healthy neurological and energetic pathways. I like to compare this process to digging a new irrigation channel or riverbed. At first it might feel a little like manual labour, but eventually the pathway is created and the energy can flow freely and naturally in a way that supports rather than sabotages you. When you've been thinking in a certain manner for a long period of time, it requires patience and practice to redirect your thoughts, words and actions consistently in a positive, healthy direction. Thus, when you find yourself doubting or rejecting a positive affirmation please know that this reaction represents a part of your psyche, personality or identity that's developed to protect you. In other words, when it's hard to accept or feel what you're affirming to be true, please be kind to yourself and know that the part of you that's resisting represents a part of you that's still hurting. In time, through being compassionate with yourself, the positive affirmations offered throughout this book will help you to heal your heart and free your mind. So please do not give up.

Practical Questions

In what ways do you suffer or struggle but hold back from sharing this with other people?

What physical symptoms or illnesses is your body expressing as a way of asking you to love and value yourself more fully?

What do you struggle to love about yourself?

What do you struggle to love about your life?

Do you ever think about killing yourself? If so, why?

Can you see how the desire to end your life is in fact a cry from your soul to heal your internal relationship with yourself? Can you see how your physical, mental and emotional pain are asking you to heal the past hurt, sadness and anger stored in your body? Can you see how you need to learn to be kind towards yourself? Can you see how you know your current habits of thinking, speaking and acting are unhealthy, and instinctually you want to transform them into new healthy ways of living? If you knew with certainty that you could be free of the pain causing your desire not to be alive, would you then want to enjoy your life? Can you please find someone to speak to about how you feel, and please talk about your suffering honestly?

Practically speaking, what can you focus your energy on today that represents you taking care of yourself and therefore honouring what you love to do, want to do or need to do?

Key Affirmations

I do not need to be sick or unhappy to be loved.

It's never too late to start over. I can re-create my life.

I am not just my thoughts or my emotions.

The voice in my head is only a small part of me.

I have everything I need within me to be healthy, happy and free.

I am willing to master loving myself unconditionally.

The loving truth inside of me will heal me and fulfil me completely.

I find strength, clarity and compassion in my suffering.

For the first time in my life I saw the truth as it is set into song by so many poets, proclaimed as the final wisdom by so many thinkers. The truth – that love is the ultimate and the highest goal to which man can aspire. Then I grasped the meaning of the greatest secret that human poetry and human thought and belief have to impart: The salvation of man is through love and in love. I understood how a man who has nothing left in this world still may know bliss, be it only for a brief moment, in the contemplation of his beloved. In a position of utter desolation, when man cannot express himself in positive action, when his only achievement may consist in enduring his sufferings in the right way – an honorable way – in such a position man can, through loving contemplation of the image he carries of his beloved, achieve fulfillment. For the first time in my life I was able to understand the meaning of the words, 'The angels are lost in perpetual contemplation of an infinite glory.'

Viktor Frankl,
Nazi concentration camp survivor,
Man's Search for Meaning

CHAPTER 3

The Search for Love

The hunger for love is much more difficult to remove than the hunger for bread.

Mother Teresa

Wherever you are, please take a few slow, deep breaths into your belly. Feel your whole body, from your feet all the way up to the crown of your head, and then down to your fingertips. Please relax any tension you feel and let yourself be. Using each inhalation to open your body and create inner space, welcome everything you're thinking, feeling and experiencing here in this moment. Please be present to your body and your breath.

Our search for love and connection is the one true driving force behind everything we do and everything we desire in life. Once our striving for approval, recognition, security or success loses its momentum, we finally realize we've simply been looking for love in all its manifestations, because when it comes down to it, what else really matters? In many cases, even before our physical survival needs for food, water or shelter have been met, our need for love surfaces as the primary motivating factor in life, because love is what makes life truly worth living. Love, and the genuine meaningful connections that arise with it, is the true medicine that heals, inspires and fulfils, and this is why, whether we're willing to admit it or not, we are either directly or indirectly in the pursuit of love right now.

This universal desire for love that we all share symbolizes a deep longing within each of us to remember who we really are and thus come home to our true nature – a nature that is, always has been and always will be an infinite source of pure love. But because we've forgotten this, most of what we do on a daily basis is motivated by our desire for others to love us or to love ourselves more fully, so that, ultimately, we can one day feel great within ourselves and our lives. Until we awaken to the source of love within, we all look for love, attention or recognition externally from others, because we haven't learned how to love and value ourselves daily in ways that are fulfilling. However, as we learn to care for ourselves emotionally and physically in practical ways, we heal the internalized hurt that blocks our access to the source of love within, and this simultaneously uncovers the love that we are. Through learning to relate to ourselves with the kindness, honesty and respect we crave, we naturally grow in our ability to embody love and thus give to others purely and unconditionally, which, along with simply enjoying each day, is an expression of our ultimate life purpose.

Your task is not to seek for love, but merely to seek and find all the barriers within yourself that you have built against it.
Jalaluddin Rumi

In our quest for healing, purpose and happiness each of us is simply looking for love. We're instinctually learning how to love ourselves and how to create healthy situations and relationships that are grounded in love. At first, we all search the outer world for the love that has its home right in our very own hearts. Each of us simply wants to be seen, understood, accepted, appreciated and valued just as we are. Deep down, we all want to feel that our lives really matter, that we're not alone, and that even a single person actually cares about our feelings, desires, needs and dreams.

The funny thing about most of us is that even though love is the one thing we all want more than anything in life, it's also the one thing that scares us more than anything else. Love scares us to our core because it requires our heart to be open and vulnerable to ourselves, to other people and to the world. We fear this love we desire so strongly because it opens our heart, and when our heart is truly naked we feel ourselves, we feel others, we feel our world, and we feel the love and the pain we've held in, closed our eyes to and disconnected from for so long.

Rather than fully feel the intensity of life, we unintentionally close our heart and cut ourselves off from the pulsating truth of what we feel because we're scared of experiencing uncomfortable emotions like rejection or insecurity that are inherent to human existence. Of course, we're not aware of this, but in doing so we actually reject our true self, which is the source of love within us. We ourselves deny ourselves access to the one thing we desire most.

We're interesting creatures, aren't we?

Fortunately, I've found that the love alive within each of us is so powerful that it will eventually transform every internal and external obstacle that stands in its way. How long this process takes depends on when we decide to face our fears and stop fighting our genuine feelings, needs and dreams. When we're finally true to ourselves each day we both stop hurting ourselves in the present and we heal past wounds, which allows the love within – the love we're looking for – to expand and fill our being.

At some point, the evolutionary impulse of life, nature and the entire universe will prevail in making sure we find this love that we're seeking. It is our destiny. But we have to learn how to be ourselves fully, and thus express the love we are through our thoughts, words and actions if we want to experience this as soon as possible. In practising this approach, life immediately improves because we prevent the pain and damage caused when we betray or hide our true self. Most importantly, we come to live each day knowing that, finally, we do not need to be more, do more or have more to be lovable, because we feel, often for the first time in our adult lives, that we are, and always have been, both lovable and abundant in love.

Ask, and it will be given to you; seek, and you will find; knock, and it will be opened to you. For everyone who asks receives, and he who seeks finds, and to him who knocks it will be opened.

Matthew 7:7–8

Unfortunately, many of us end up making ourselves sick or depressed because we don't know how else to get the love, attention, support, rest or space for ourselves that we need. We're still waiting on others to give us what we didn't receive as children and never learned to give to ourselves. The truth is you do not need to be ill or unhappy to get love, support or time to care for yourself. You can give it to yourself. But first you have to acknowledge that you never learned how to clearly express what you feel or to ask for what you need. We all learned a very self-destructive way of getting love, attention and support, which not only destroys us if we don't heal it, but also covers the internal source we're looking to unlock.

You do not need to break down physically or mentally before it's okay to talk about your emotions or to take personal time to care for yourself. It's okay to attend to yourself now, before seeking love, attention or security externally makes you feel worse than you do today. If you don't give yourself space and permission to understand this truth within you, it makes it hard to find or attract the true love, connection, peace or happiness you're seeking. There is a path to feeling enough, to feeling lovable, and to reconnecting to the source of love within you. But this path challenges you to accept that it is possible to be loved for who you are, as you are, rather than for what you do for others or for how much you please them.

Practical Questions

What do you love most in life and about life?

What are all of the little things that you love?

What are your favourite things to do, see, taste, touch, smell, experience, feel, create or accomplish?

What makes you happy?

What activities bring out your happiness?

What has made you happy in the past?

Whom do you love in your life? Whom do you truly care about and value?

Whom do you expect to make you happy or satisfy you?

Whom do you constantly try to please, make happy or satisfy?

What would happen if you stopped?

What can you focus your energy on today that represents you caring for yourself and therefore honouring what you love to do, want to do or need to do?

Key Affirmations

My soul is made of pure love.

I am pure, unconditional love.

There is an ocean of love inside of me.

I am one with the infinite universe.

I do not need to search outside of myself for love.

I am enough.

I am lovable just as I am.

I do not need to be more, do more or have more to love myself
or to be loved by others.

CHAPTER 4

Healthy Selfishness

A person who seeks help for a friend, while needy himself, will be answered first.

The Talmud

Wherever you are, please take a few slow, deep breaths into your belly. Feel your whole body, from your feet all the way up to the crown of your head, and then down to your fingertips. Please relax any tension you feel and let yourself be. Using each inhalation to open your body and create inner space, welcome everything you're thinking, feeling and experiencing here in this moment. Please be present to your body and your breath.

If you're honest with yourself, would you say you're a selfish person or a selfless person? What do you think of the assertion that everyone is in fact selfish, regardless of how well it is masked? Could you entertain the view that some of us are healthy in our selfish tendencies while most of us are quite unhealthy and destructive, which is what gives the topic of 'selfishness' a negative association and leads us to deny it as a fundamental attribute of human nature?

If you really analyse it, you will eventually see that we either take good care of ourselves – which enables us actually to have time and energy for others – or we neglect our mental, emotional and physical wellbeing, and therefore live in the world with stress, resentment and a lack of joy. Our metaphorical cup is either overflowing from constructive thoughts, emotions and healthy lifestyle habits, arising from selfishly attending to our deeper feelings and needs, or it is devoid of anything positive to offer because it has become full of toxicity after years of self-destructive compromise, emotional repression and fear-based living.

Nature was actually designed to thrive through a healthy and selfish form of self-preservation whereby an organism finds what it needs first to survive and eventually to thrive in balance with its environment. A wonderful example of this is an apple tree, which could not offer oxygen for us to breathe, apples for us to eat or shade for us to find shelter beneath if it did not selfishly absorb the water and nutrients from the earth or the light and energy from the sun that it needs to grow strong and healthy. Being an integral part of nature, we too were designed to function optimally through this same form of healthy self-interest. As a human being, not only does our body, heart and mind function best when we give ourselves what we need to be well, happy and strong, but the natural by-product of this dynamic is that we also have much more to give to others when we have truly attended to ourselves.

Self-care is never a selfish act – it is simply good stewardship of the only gift I have, the gift I was put on earth to offer to others.

Parker Palmer

When you read the phrase *healthy selfishness* you might think these two words contradict each other or you may recognize the limiting belief you inherited from your parents or from society that being selfish is negative, bad, wrong, unhealthy or sinful. Many people who read this may recognize they have created their entire life based on a fear of being judged as selfish. If you fall into this category where you have spent, or still spend, the majority of your life pleasing others and putting yourself either second or last when dealing with your family, friends, partner or spouse, the truth is you are still selfish in your ways. You have simply learned a very unhealthy and self-destructive form of selfishness, which is currently masked in your perception as selflessness or martyrdom, but which in reality is your completely selfish way of surviving and getting what you want and think you need.

Our fears often cause us to selfishly protect ourselves and remain comfortable rather than face the criticism of those closest to us. It's common to keep denying what we really feel, want or need because we're scared of the reactions and the responsibilities that will come with speaking or acting based on our inner truth. When we learn to be honest with ourselves and with others, the people who are used to us pleasing them will become faced instead with their own anger, hurt and insecurity, which our pleasing behaviours have temporarily masked. When we honour ourselves without always pacifying others, we also run the risk of being rejected by those we love and value most, because anyone who still compromises and betrays themselves regularly will find it hard to understand our growing sense of self-respect and self-worth. They may unintentionally judge us, but only because they are still judging themselves for not exercising the courage to value themselves.

The ultimate example I like to use to deconstruct the myth of selflessness, and one that proves that everyone is in fact selfish, is that of a parent. If we truly question every possible reason for a woman or man to bring a child into this world, we find strictly selfish motives. No woman or man says I want to have a child and give up the next twenty-plus years of my life to meet the needs of someone who will most likely take me for granted, and then blame me for all their problems. I frame it in this light a bit humorously to make a point, but, with the utmost respect, this is a very sensitive and confronting fact for some people.

Since anyone who reads this is obviously the child of their

parents, please pause for a moment here and ask yourself why your parents conceived you and then birthed you into this world? Was this motivating factor selfish or selfless? If you yourself want to be a parent, are now a parent or have been for years, please also pause to ask yourself why you want children or had children in the first place? If you're as honest with yourself as possible, have your motives been selfless or selfish?

Whether parenthood was a conscious choice or an accident, it is the best example of selfishness disguised as selfless sacrifice, because men and women always create children from their own desire to do so, even if parenting ends up being different to what they thought it would be. In other words, any person who has a child does so because it's their dream to have a family, or it's their intention to parent better than their parents did, or to give a child what they never received. Although rarely admitted, many times a child is an unwanted mistake, for one or both parents, who were simply wanting to have fun, or to enjoy the pleasures of sexual intimacy, or seeking the love, approval or acceptance of the opposite sex. In some cases, a woman or a man doesn't know what else to do with their life and so having a child seems like a good option, because – why not – everyone else is doing it. Sometimes having a child is a compromise to keep a man, or not to lose a woman, or to become financially secure, or to escape one's own parents, or to change one's life, or in some sad cases, an opportunity for a larger benefit payment from the government. In other words, even the most loving, giving and apparently 'self-sacrificing' parent is selfish.

What we all need to acknowledge, besides our selfish nature, is that there is nothing wrong with this fact because it's the way life is. The key point here is that it's healthier to be honest about your own selfishness as well as that of others, so that you can make informed choices based on deep self-love and truth. It's actually better for everyone that we stop making self-destructive decisions that are based on denial or the lies we tell ourselves. The more we understand and accept this, the clearer it becomes that when we do love ourselves in healthy ways we're actually preparing ourselves to give consciously to other people, without there being manipulation, conditions or strings attached.

Giving time, energy or support to others, even to our own detriment, often feels so natural, because spiritually speaking, there is no true separation between anyone. So, when we love others we are also loving ourselves. However, on a practical level, most of us unintentionally focus on others as a means of distracting ourselves from our deeper feelings, needs and desires, because we've never learned how to simply be alone with our thoughts and emotions. We often try to make other people happy and we assert our motives are selfless, when in reality we don't know how to say 'no' and we also expect others to please us in similar ways. When they do not, we feel hurt, resentful or used, because we were in fact 'giving to get' instead of giving from a pure, full and selfless place. Most forms of blame arise from this habit of relating that we think is morally 'good' or socially acceptable. Having learned the very common unhealthy form of selfishness, we unintentionally neglect ourselves, thinking this is both normal and healthy. But the truth is we don't know any better, because most of us never learned how to meet our own needs or to ask for what we want. Instead, we hide our selfish tendencies and our giving to others unintentionally becomes manipulative.

Fear is the greatest obstacle to turning our unhealthy selfish tendencies into a form of healthy selfishness that first benefits us and then later benefits everyone we know and meet. Fear of hurting others, fear of owning the hurt we have caused, fear of being judged, fear of being rejected, fear of being vulnerable, fear of losing love, fear of losing support, fear of losing a partner, spouse or friend, and fear of being alone are some of the most common ways we justify our self-destructive tendencies. But, as a result, we end up relating to ourselves in harmful ways, which then become unhealthy and destructive for the people around us as well. From this objective perspective, which approach is optimal in your mind?

A simple example of this is a partner or parent who never acts for themselves directly, but rather pleases others all the time and puts themselves last or second. This typically results in resentment, frustration and dissatisfaction, and in my experience, eventually leads to depression, relationship problems and various forms of physical illness. Another common example of this is a person who is addicted to drugs or alcohol because they do not know how to address their deeper emotions, needs or desires. Their unhealthy selfish tendency of numbing themselves and avoiding their real wounds then becomes harmful to the people around them. Their toxic inner world overflows and becomes toxic for everyone involved. If, however, they could learn to love and value themselves enough to address their true feelings, they would then want to take better care of their body and their life overall. They would feel they matter and have worth.

There is a huge misunderstanding around the term *selfish* because we are so familiar with its unhealthy manifestation. Healthy selfishness does not mean we become cold, insensitive, rude or always alone. Being selfish in a healthy way does not mean we disregard other people's feelings and needs. It simply means we do not harm ourselves to please others or to support others like so many of us do. It means we take care of our body and value our feelings, needs and dreams, which then renders us capable of respecting this healthy desire in other people. Contrary to how most people think, as we learn to be selfish in healthy ways we actually become more compassionate and understanding, because rather than expecting others to meet our needs or please us all the time, we realize that other people have their own feelings, needs and desires that they must attend to each day for them to be healthy and happy as well. Although many of us were raised to believe otherwise, it is not wrong to desire health and happiness. It is not immoral to be the best person you can be. It is not sinful to live your life to the fullest. Rather it is healthy.

Not only is it okay to selfishly pursue activities, experiences, relationships and a career that bring you joy and make you feel well, it is also vital to finding inner peace and to making the world a more peaceful place. If we settle for less than we're capable of, or for less good than we know is possible in life, we'll just be resentful, sad and ill, which is not good for anyone. Believing you are selfless, or playing the role of a martyr, but ending up sick and miserable, in no way serves the world.

CHAPTER 5

Healing Guilt, Shame and Insecurity

It is no measure of health to be well adjusted to a profoundly sick society.

Jiddu Krishnamurti

Wherever you are, please take a few slow, deep breaths into your belly. Feel your whole body, from your feet all the way up to the crown of your head, and then down to your fingertips. Please relax any tension you feel and let yourself be. Using each inhalation to open your body and create inner space, welcome everything you're thinking, feeling and experiencing here in this moment. Please be present to your body and your breath.

Do you constantly make yourself wrong for feeling the way you feel or for desiring the things you desire in life? Do you find yourself feeling guilty after you express your emotions or after doing something just for yourself that's not about pleasing someone else? Do you constantly fear hurting others when making a choice that's best for you, but then find that you stop yourself and hurt yourself instead? If you answered yes to any of these questions, then you're just like me and most people on the planet who suffer with deep guilt whereby we not only feel that we are a problem – that our mere existence is a burden – but also that we are somehow wrong, bad or sinful for wanting to be happy, well and truly loved.

Is the fact that we're surviving really enough? Should we just accept that it's 'normal' to live in fear, with deep insecurity, shame and anxiety? Is asking to thrive, to achieve your dreams, to feel completely satisfied in your intimate relationship, or to realize your full potential personally and professionally, really too much to ask? My personal view is that you and I did not come here just to survive or to settle for crumbs of happiness, peace, health or love. Rather, we're all destined to learn how to value ourselves enough not to settle for less than a whole loaf in each area. It is not wrong to want to enjoy our life, our relationships and our body. It is not wrong to desire fulfilling work that has meaning, but which also pays the bills, puts food on the table and eventually provides the financial freedom for us never to feel trapped somewhere we don't want to be.

I have found that there is a golden thread to much of our suffering, which once understood helps us to heal the origin of insecurity, fear, guilt and shame. The root cause of these emotions that so many of us battle with daily goes back to our conception, our time in our mother's womb and our early childhood. Please think back to what life might have been like for your mother and father when they made love, or had sex, and thus created you. Do you think your parents were deeply self-aware, emotionally or financially stable, happy in themselves, masterful at loving themselves, or truly satisfied in their intimate relationship? It has become very obvious to me, having worked with thousands of people in all phases of life, that most people are stressed, spread thin, confused, scared, or do not know who they are, to varying degrees of course, when they bring a life into the world.

Some people are aware of this internal unrest while others are very good at repressing what they feel and thus carry on as though everything is okay, when in reality there's quite a bit of inner turmoil present. The relevance of this fact comes into play when we stop to consider that we not only absorb everything that our mother eats and drinks while she is pregnant, but we also inherit much of what she believes, thinks, feels and experiences in her environment. If Mum is insecure, confused, scared or anxious, then we will most likely be born with these energies alive within us. Likewise, if Mum is confident, at peace and feeling supported in life, we will most likely feel this way too. The same is true of how and where our biological father is in himself at the time of our conception, birth and in our early formative years. If Dad is scared, stressed or absent, we will feel this. If he is excited, clear and committed, then we'll feel this too.

The bridge between this fact and why we make ourselves wrong so much is that most of our parents felt at some point that having children was stressful, a sacrifice or burdensome. Even though no parent would ever choose to feel this way, let alone admit to it, it is a very common fact based on the truth that we are inherently selfish creatures. We can sense this unspoken truth while growing up and it's intimately tied up with every other repressed truth that eventually leads to various forms of suffering later in life. This in no way means our parents were bad people, nor does it mean you're wrong for feeling this way if you're a parent. Exploring these facts is not about judging our parents or judging ourselves. It's not about blaming anyone either. What this perspective offers is an objective awareness of one major cause of our struggles, which needs to be understood and healed if we want to be healthy and happy in the long run.

If you reflect back on your childhood and then fast-forward to today, contemplating on your relationship with your parents, you may well recognize that you've always felt like a problem. Some may feel that their decisions, needs, feelings, desires and innocent imaginings were not welcomed and supported, but rather judged, shut down or ignored. Others may feel this was not the case for them, or may struggle to understand how this would apply to them personally. Even if you feel your parents gave you a lot of love, you still would have developed habits to please them or not upset them, which once again results in you rejecting aspects of what you feel, need or want, in exchange for love. Insecurity, guilt, shame and fear *always* co-arise with this dynamic.

For all of us, especially those of us who clearly felt like a burden or were blatantly unwanted, it is very liberating to understand how we developed a deep insecurity and lack of self-worth because we felt that our physical and emotional life was a problem growing up. Even though it can be hard to swallow, somewhere deep in the subconscious we all feel some degree of guilt today just for existing, which is tied up with our guilt and shame for having feelings, needs, desires and dreams. This is where we really learn to repress and hide what's going on for us out of a fear of being abandoned, rejected, criticized or abused. It's also where we learn to feel insecure about losing the often-toxic love and attention we're being given. Viewed in this light, it's easy to see why as adults we keep going back to unhealthy relationships or situations. Early in life we were conditioned to rely on one source of love, security or connection that may have been very cold, toxic, abusive or twisted in some way, so we became used to this way of relating, which is how we learned to settle for it in our adult life.

If you are starving for love, and you're only getting crumbs, naturally you're going to become very scared of losing the small amount of nourishment coming your way. Further, until you know better, you will do whatever it takes to keep those crumbs. Because we depend on our parents or our caregivers as vulnerable children – regardless of how healthy or unhealthy they were – we learn to avoid saying or doing things that might cause them to withdraw the typically small amounts of love and support we're receiving. Then there are some of us who simply didn't want to be verbally, physically or sexually abused, so we shut down to keep the little peace we might have found. Although we cannot articulate it, this is also where we learned to feel we don't matter or have any value – especially when our adult caregivers were insensitive, stressed, aggressive or completely absent. First, we don't learn how to understand or express our feelings, and then, second, we learn to deny these inner truths simply to get by, which becomes a very self-destructive habit that now defines the life of many of us as adults. We are unintentionally made wrong by our parents, caregivers or teachers early on, and then we learn to make ourselves wrong for feeling what we feel, for needing what we need, for wanting what we want, or for dreaming what we imagine.

Since our parents had us for selfish reasons, the logical and objective truth is that most of them had no idea what raising children would require, nor were they ready for the responsibility. Having a family, putting food on the table, maintaining a healthy partnership, and finding some peace and happiness is not easy for anyone. It is stressful. But even so, practically speaking, it's important to understand that this is directly related to how, where and why so many of us developed an unhealthy relationship to ourselves in which we make ourselves wrong in exchange for the unhealthy and conditional love, approval, acceptance or support of others. It is a self-destructive pattern that our parents learned from their parents and it is tied up with all the insecurity, guilt, shame and fear that has been passed down genetically, emotionally and habitually for generations.

In my professional experience, and also as a man who has personally struggled to heal my own deep insecurities, I've found that understanding this dynamic is the one thread to uprooting the source of insecurity, guilt, shame and also physical disease. As children we didn't know how to give ourselves permission to be true to ourselves in every situation, but now we can master this. As adults it's very common to fear being rejected and abandoned because we subconsciously feared being rejected as children. From the very beginning of life we learned to choose between our own happiness and pleasing others. It seemed we could not have both. We all learned to fear hurting others, so we hurt ourselves instead. We learned to fear saying no to others, so now we neglect ourselves. Understanding this deep block that keeps so many of us stuck, miserable or sick is key to overcoming it because once we're truly aware of this dynamic we can never forget it completely. This reality is not anyone's fault, but rather something we need to be mindful of now if we want to break the self-destructive cycle and stop settling for crumbs of love, health, happiness and respect.

CHAPTER 6

Value Yourself

The hardest challenge is to be yourself in a world where everyone is trying to make you be somebody else.

E E Cummings

Wherever you are, please take a few slow, deep breaths into your belly. Feel your whole body, from your feet all the way up to the crown of your head, and then down to your fingertips. Please relax any tension you feel and let yourself be. Using each inhalation to open your body and create inner space, welcome everything you're thinking, feeling and experiencing here in this moment. Please be present to your body and your breath.

It's often not until we allow other people to treat us horribly and therefore feel worthless or valueless that we realize our approach to life truly needs to change. Unfortunately, things have to get seriously bad, painful or out of control for most of us before we realize how important it is to honour and value ourselves consistently in every moment, situation and relationship. For those of us who often feel inadequate, insecure, undeserving or unworthy of love, we will constantly abandon and betray ourselves for the love of others to the point where we repeatedly find ourselves in situations where we feel used, unappreciated, valueless or worthless to those around us as well as to ourselves. Underneath these painful situations, however, is the empowering truth that we're not actually victims in any way. We're actually the ones who've compromised ourselves for the conditional acceptance, approval, attention and support of other people and thus we can change this self-destructive pattern. We can make a different choice now.

What most of us don't realize until we've allowed our own sense of self-worth and self-respect to reach zero is that in every moment we do not value ourselves, we are abandoning and hurting ourselves far more deeply than we know. This hurt that we unconsciously inflict upon ourselves then creates deep anger, shame, frustration, resentment, hatred and dissatisfaction within us that we hold towards ourselves. In every moment we're either being true to ourselves or we're compromising ourselves. So in each situation that we allow our fears of losing love, acceptance, approval, attention, security or support to determine our choices and actions, we add to the build-up of pain, sadness and inner dis-ease that we've already created for ourselves by betraying ourselves so much throughout our lives.

As we touched on in the last chapter, most of us never felt safe enough as children to fully be ourselves or to express everything we feel, think, want or need. As a result, our instincts led all of us to fragment ourselves in exchange for the conditional love we felt we needed from our parents, our teachers, our peers and our caregivers just to survive. These deep fears that we all carry forward to some degree then lead us to betray ourselves as adults. Whether it's with our parents, our children, other family members, our spouse, our partner, our friends, our colleagues, our employers or our employees, most of us still abandon our inner truths in exchange for something.

This soul-destroying exchange might come in the form of wanting to fit in, to avoid confrontation, to be accepted, to attract attention, to be approved of, to feel safe or to have financial security. It may also come in the form of desiring fame, companionship, pleasure or sex. Regardless of who or what we've compromised ourselves for over the years, a large number of us have created a completely compromised life because we didn't know better and we never learned how to break through our fears of losing love and security to always be true to who we genuinely are.

Feeling unlovable or undeserving of love, just as we are, is no way to live. But there's a grey area in our psyche and heart where we feel valueless or worthless, and it needs to be healed for us to be happy and well. This blind spot in our awareness drives many of us to stay in situations, relationships and jobs that do not reflect our true feelings, ultimately because we hold the destructive belief that no one else will stand by us, love us or employ us if we genuinely value ourselves. It's heart-breaking that so many of us live believing that we lack something within ourselves, which renders us unworthy of love, happiness and respect. Even though this is completely untrue, we still end up hurting ourselves because we feel the only way to be loved, accepted, approved of or supported by other people or by a business is to please them and make them happy, even if it's at the expense of our own integrity, happiness or wellbeing.

This self-destructive pattern of relating to ourselves leads us to live out the majority of our days disregarding our own values and needs for this tainted form of love. This is how our lives become a constant struggle to please others while deep down we remain tense, bitter, alone and unsatisfied. What we fail to realize is that simply by valuing ourselves in each situation, starting now, we can heal our core inadequacies and insecurities and eventually discover that we've always been worthy of all things good, nourishing and beautiful.

Be soft. Do not let the world make you hard. Do not let
pain make you hate. Do not let the bitterness steal your
sweetness. Take pride that even though the rest of the world
may disagree, you still believe it to be a beautiful place.

Kurt Vonnegut

Learning to value the very deepest parts of ourselves is often
a painful stage in our awakening, through which we finally
claim the intrinsic worth of our lives in and of themselves.
Regardless of how it appears from the outside, we all live
with parts of ourselves that are like dark rooms in which
fragments of our soul feel mistreated or abandoned, and it
seems as though no one is listening to our pain-filled cries.
Ironically, it is ourselves whom we're calling out to, asking
our higher self to turn on the lights and flood these dark
spaces within us with a deep self-love, care and respect.
When we've lived believing and feeling that we're not
lovable or deserving of love, we find that there exists a
number of these 'dark rooms' or 'blind spots' within us that
are devoid of self-value and self-worth. As we touched on
before, it's often not until we allow ourselves to be used or
taken advantage of that we realize that we are in fact the
ones who have somehow betrayed ourselves.

If we still need to master this lesson, then each day we
will purposefully create situations where we invite people
into our lives to exploit us or test us, which reveals the
wounded parts of ourselves that are still hurting and waiting
to be rescued by our own loving care. Through our desires
for peace, health, happiness and authentic connection our
soul calls us home and asks us to turn on the lights in these
parts of ourselves so we can assert from deep inside our
being that *we do not want to allow or create any more suffering*

for ourselves. Once we finally make this assertion, courage begins to arise within us so we can stand strong and flood these once darkened spaces with a knowing that we've always deserved genuine love, kindness and respect.

It's helpful to know that these parts of ourselves that are temporarily devoid of awareness and love are the sole causes for the situations in our lives where we do not feel valued, appreciated or respected by other people. If we don't value and respect ourselves, the people around us will mirror this back. If we don't matter to ourselves, then our feelings, needs and desires won't matter to those around us either. Once we finally commit to enlightening these love-deprived spaces within us, we're called to honour our true feelings in every aspect of our personal and professional lives. This unavoidable process of re-creating our inner relationship with ourselves is often one of the most difficult aspects of our ongoing healing and spiritual journey, because it requires us to value ourselves enough to either re-create or leave behind every situation that does not mirror back our newfound self-respect and self-worth.

On a practical level, honouring ourselves means saying no sometimes; it often means we stand strongly in our truth, with kindness, respect and vulnerability, and then face whatever reactions arise when we do not speak and act merely to please others or to make them happy. Sometimes valuing ourselves means we need to leave a relationship, a job or a certain place, knowing deep down that our daily integrity, health and happiness are more important than the safety and security of cold, heartless, financial or material comfort.

I have observed that once we've suffered enough and are thus ready to value ourselves without compromising our inner truths for anyone or anything, life and the universe will always step up to help us on our destined path. We cannot know exactly how circumstances will unfold to provide us with precisely what we need to move forward, but we can always be certain that we'll be supported in fulfilling our life's purpose to bring love, joy and truth into the world. The opportunities, emotional help, financial resources and clarity we need do arise with each courageous step we take into the unknown territory of deep self-respect.

Practical Questions

Where and with whom in your life right now are you compromising yourself and abandoning your inner truth, in any way, for love, acceptance, approval, companionship, emotional support, financial support, safety or security?

Why are you compromising, abandoning and betraying yourself?

With whom in your life do you struggle to say no? Why do you struggle to say no?

Who in your life do you feel you must always please, satisfy or make happy?

Have you ever felt abandoned by anyone? If so, can you see how you had abandoned yourself or your feelings, needs and desires somehow in the relationship? Can you see how this subconscious pattern has most likely been recurring since your childhood?

Where in your life are you settling for less than you know you are worthy, deserving or capable of? Why are you settling for this?

What do you want and need for yourself and your life that you're neglecting?

What can you do on a daily basis that represents you taking the time to consistently honour, value and love yourself?

Key Affirmations

I do not need to compromise myself for love.

It's okay for me to say no and honour what I feel, need and want.

I do not need to be more, do more or have more for others to love me.

I am lovable just the way I am.

I am enough. I am not lacking in anything.

I deserve to be honoured, valued and appreciated.

I am worthy and deserving of love.

I will not settle for less than I am worthy, deserving or capable of.

I will not abandon or betray myself ever again.

CHAPTER 7

How to Be Yourself

Some of us think holding on makes us strong,
but sometimes it is letting go.

Hermann Hesse

Wherever you are, please take a few slow, deep breaths into your belly. Feel your whole body, from your feet all the way up to the crown of your head, and then down to your fingertips. Please relax any tension you feel and let yourself be. Using each inhalation to open your body and create inner space, welcome everything you're thinking, feeling and experiencing here in this moment. Please be present to your body and your breath.

If you stop pretending to be something you are not, or to feel other than you do, then what? If you were to let your mask come off, and show the world all of who you really are, then who would we all get to meet? If you stopped trying to fit in or to please your parents, friends, partner or whomever else's approval, praise or love you seek, then what would you say? Where would you go? And what would you do?

If you allowed the world to see your darkness and your light, your vulnerability and your power, do you fear you'd end up alone? But wait, are you not alone already when you feel misunderstood or unable to express what you really think and feel?

It is ironic that we as human beings inevitably have to ask ourselves, 'How do I be myself?' One might assume that it's easy and natural to be ourselves, yet so many of us have become disconnected from our true self that the opposite now seems to be the case. It seems easier to be something for someone else, or to please others, or to fit in, rather than risk standing out or being judged.

It becomes both practical and logical then, to ask, 'Who am I?' Who are YOU? Are you your body? Your mind? The thoughts in your head? Are you your emotions? Are you the visual image you see in your mind or the list of beliefs that make up the fabric of your identity?

Are you your past, or the story you tell to describe how you got to where you are today? Are you your future? Or the person you envisage yourself becoming, or dream to be?

Who are you really?

In my experience, if you want to be happy, it is crucial for you to ask this question and answer it for yourself, rather than taking my word or anyone else's. What I can share, in the hope that it might help you to find your own inner knowing, are the answers I found for myself when asking this question.

Here it's also important to state again that words can never do the truth justice. They are our best attempt at communicating what we feel and experience, but this is ultimately, and always, far beyond words. Words are not the truth in and of itself. Rather they are arrows or signposts pointing towards a felt understanding of a given experience or aspect of being human. They form a map, which may very accurately describe the terrain, but it is still not the terrain itself.

In my own quest to understand who I am, using language as accurately as I am able, I have come to the conclusions below. At first these may seem ungrounded, but please be patient, because I intend to take you from universal ultimate truths about who we are into practical facts about how to be ourselves.

1. I am; meaning that I exist, as an aggregate of my non-physical and physical self. This includes my physical body, my thinking mind, the emotions I experience within my heart and body, the breath/oxygen that fills

my lungs, and the life-force energy that animates my physical being with vitality, personality and conscious awareness. However, ultimately, all of these are just attributes of one whole, which is who I am, beyond words, division, concepts or boxes. An example of this would be a tree, which has leaves, branches and possibly fruit, but which we typically just call a *tree*. However, once again, please keep in mind that the word *tree*, even though all of us know what I am referring to, still is not the same as seeing, touching, smelling or sitting beneath an actual tree. Nor do we have any clue how the tree experiences itself.

2. I am one with the universe, including all energy (atoms), matter, forms of life and nature, inanimate objects and space.

3. I am one with the creative intelligence and awareness that created and sustains the existence of the universe (sometimes called God, depending on your belief system).

4. I am infinite, immortal and eternal, in that my being is composed of energy and consciousness that cannot be created or destroyed. In other words, I was never really born, nor will I ever die. I merely took form as a human being at a point in space-time, and I have no idea what form I will take next once my physical self stops functioning and returns to dust. What I do know is that I will return to the vast ocean of energy that makes up the universe in both its physical and non-physical forms.

Some people like to use the words soul and spirit when describing this timeless aspect of ourselves. I like these words as well, but they are not necessary to describe who I am, or who you are. From this perspective, though, the universe is the soul of God, or everything and everyone within the universe is the universe's soul unfolding into different forms. This means that our soul or spirit is one with the universe's or God's soul. I love this metaphor and perspective but, once again, it's not necessary to believe this in order to be yourself and be happy.

5. I am love, in that I feel the most alive, well and like myself when I am in a state of love, whereby I can give and receive love freely, without fear. I also feel most like myself when I am engaged in activities that I love deeply, which bring out my essence, which is love that is happy doing and being itself.

Practically speaking, being ourselves entails more than just conceptually understanding our true nature. It entails becoming sufficiently self-aware in the present to express ourselves in a way whereby we naturally and effectively communicate our emotions, needs and desires on a daily basis, instead of hiding, denying, rejecting and internalizing them. Most of us struggle with this step, primarily because we were never supported to become aware of our emotional life as children. We grew up with emotions bottled up, without anyone to help us understand or process what we were feeling because our parents and caregivers were struggling with the same lack of emotional self-awareness. The result of this dynamic is adults who are not consciously aware of what they are feeling today, which translates into not knowing how to express these emotions, let alone communicate them effectively and non-violently. In other words, before we can express our emotions clearly, we have to be aware of what we're feeling here in the present, which most of us are not. Rather, we are trapped in our mind thinking, analysing, judging or criticizing, which means that the defensive aspects of our personality that developed to protect us as children are still very active. Regardless of our age, most of us still subconsciously want to remain safe both from being hurt in the present and from feeling the stored hurt from the past.

This makes it easy to see how and why so many of us struggle to be ourselves and thus be happy, because to be ourselves we have to be true to ourselves, which means we have to speak and act based on what we genuinely feel to be honest and real in each situation. But, if we do not know what we're feeling, we cannot express it and thus cannot be ourselves fully. However, once we do become aware of our feelings, needs and desires in the here and now, we can honour who we truly are and learn to express our inner truths with clarity and kindness.

CHAPTER 8

Express Yourself Clearly and Kindly

Be who you are and say what you feel, because those who mind don't matter and those who matter don't mind.

Dr Seuss

Wherever you are, please take a few slow, deep breaths into your belly. Feel your whole body, from your feet all the way up to the crown of your head, and then down to your fingertips. Please relax any tension you feel and let yourself be. Using each inhalation to open your body and create inner space, welcome everything you're thinking, feeling and experiencing here in this moment. Please be present to your body and your breath.

In addition to our fears of losing love, many of us developed a pattern of internalizing our emotions because it didn't seem to make a difference to anyone whether or not we spoke up. A number of us just gave up on expressing ourselves long before we were even equipped with the tools or the language to do so effectively. In reaction to our early experiences, most of us have lived our whole adult lives replaying childhood patterns of relating to the people around us. For many of us here in the present, it seems as though no one cares about what we think or feel, when in reality we never learned how to express ourselves clearly. Although we're often not aware of this, the people in our lives are struggling with the exact same issues around expressing themselves, because they too never learned how to do so in healthy ways. Knowing this, if we want our own feelings, needs and dreams to matter to the people currently in our lives, these inner realities must first matter to us, regardless of how they're received. In the present, we are called to value everything that arises within us before we can attract people into our lives who genuinely want to understand us and know us at the depths of our heart and soul.

Regardless of the stage of life we're presently in, internalizing what we think, feel, want or need in any moment out of fear or simple unawareness is one of the most self-destructive patterns that we hold. As we've explored it is the root cause of depression and most forms of physical disease. In order to maintain a healthy and balanced flow of energy, blood and emotion in our body, we have to learn to welcome all of what we think and feel and then express ourselves mindfully with personal responsibility. If we want to feel well, enjoy life and fulfil our purpose, we have to learn to express ourselves without allowing our fears of losing love, being judged or upsetting others to stop us. Even when we're feeling confused or unclear about how we feel, it's still better to open up and communicate our feelings, because it's only through expressing ourselves that we find the clarity and understanding that's necessary to move forward. Just like a rusty water tap that hasn't been used for a long time, we have to flush out the blockages and muddled energies in our own expression channels before we can consistently communicate our thoughts and feelings in conscious, clear and mutually respectful ways.

Raise your words, not your voice. It is rain that grows flowers, not thunder.

Jalaluddin Rumi

Learning to express ourselves fully also entails taking responsibility for how we react when we feel that we're not being heard. A number of us tend to yell and scream when we feel that what we're saying or trying to communicate is not being valued. When we aim to cultivate deep self-love and respect, we're faced with the task of mastering the process of expressing what we think and feel in non-violent and unaggressive ways. This undertaking presents a deep challenge for many of us who grew up around people who used angry reactions and emotional manipulation as a means to control various situations and thus avoid personal responsibility. Learning to be accountable for what we think and feel while simultaneously expressing ourselves with awareness, respect and kindness might be one of the most difficult lessons life presents to us, especially since we tend to take on the same unconscious patterns of emotional manipulation in our own lives that we were witness to growing up.

What's crucial to understand here is that underneath all the moments in which we feel the need to scream or yell to be heard, and underneath all the moments in which we've witnessed those we care about scream or yell to get a point across, the truth is that we're all hurting in our hearts and have never consciously learned how to express what we feel. Our angry reactions and the aggressive behaviours that result are merely our unconscious ways of protecting ourselves from past emotional pain that we've never felt safe enough or supported enough to feel and express. To make matters worse, on top of never learning how to express ourselves in kind and responsible ways, most of us learned a way of speaking to each other that is aggressive and full of blame. Rather than learning to respectfully say, 'I think', 'I feel', 'I want', or 'I need' so and so, we learned to point the finger at others and say things like 'You' this or 'You' that or 'You're such a ...' or 'You never ...', etc. We learned a form of communication that very effectively breeds hurt, defensiveness and separation as opposed to open communication, trust, understanding, mutual respect and deep connection.

The result of this painful cycle that's been passed

down from generation to generation is people who are constantly crying out to be heard, valued, respected and loved. Thankfully, however, there's a very simple solution to this age-old problem. We merely have to own the fact that we're not only one hundred per cent responsible for what we think and feel, but also one hundred per cent responsible for valuing it, by expressing ourselves from a place of vulnerable honesty, kindness and respect. If we can accept that underneath all our angry emotional reactions, both spoken and thought, there's simply a part of us that's hurting and thus protecting us from further pain, we can finally allow ourselves to heal our emotional and psychic wounds. Below every screaming match or aggressive form of communication, there's a little boy or girl who's crying out for the unconditional love and support of his or her mother and/or father. When we can see ourselves and others in this penetrating light, we cannot help but open our heart and express ourselves in kind, sensitive ways that lead to healing, happiness and connection instead of further pain and feelings of isolation.

Regardless of how much verbal abuse or aggression we've either witnessed or taken part in, deep down we all want to express ourselves clearly and lovingly, so that we feel heard, validated and respected daily. We all want to feel that the people in our lives care enough to want to understand us in the depths of our heart and soul. No one wants to feel constantly made wrong or criticized. What most of us fail to realize – and thus fail to take responsibility for – is that we ourselves have to care enough about ourselves to value, respect and express what we're truly feeling before we can expect to create or attract relationships that consistently meet us in the deep ways we all intuitively desire. We have to stop making ourselves wrong and listen to our heart's most subtle and scary truths, because this is the only way to be intimately connected to ourselves, which is a prerequisite to ever being intimately connected to other human beings in healthy ways.

Practically speaking, when we internalize what we feel, we fragment ourselves and cut ourselves off from the source of what we're seeking. The direct and immediate result of this are feelings of not being good enough or of lacking in some way. Our body is like a hose that's connected to the ocean, but the hose has become kinked and knotted up, which cuts off the flow and makes it appear as though there's a lack of water. But the truth is that after years of not expressing ourselves we've simply clogged up and twisted our connection to the source of everything we need. Thankfully, as soon as we break the dam and begin speaking our truth with loving-kindness, we instantly start to feel both whole and worthy of love. We're finally allowing ourselves to be our authentic self which is the primary ingredient for deep healing, health and happiness.

Once we face our fears and start speaking kindly and honestly in each situation, we begin bridging the gap in our perception between our small insecure self and our confident true self that knows who we are and why we were born. Although it might seem absurd, I have found that each word spoken from truth and love, from our heart through our mouth, is a primary factor in generating the energy and immunity needed to heal from within. It's like a medicinal balm that mends and strengthens us from the inside out.

Our authentic self-expression is a manifestation of inner health and emotional intelligence, and it is this way of being that first helps us personally, but then expands out to help our loved ones and our world.

Practical Questions

Where and with whom in your life right now do you struggle to express what you think, feel, want and need?

Where and with whom in the past have you struggled to express your inner truths?

Who in your life right now do you fear being honest with?

Are you afraid of upsetting them, hurting them, or losing their love and support?

What are you *feeling* right now in your body?

What do you truly *want* in your life right now, both internally and externally?

What do you *need* right now?

Do you have anyone with whom you can *share* this?
If not, can you write about this?

Key Affirmations

I express my truth and trust that all will be okay.

I forgive myself for not expressing myself in the past.

I do not need to fear punishment. I'm not a child any more.

Expressing my emotions is the path to health, happiness
and fulfilment.

I express my needs and desires with love, respect
and awareness.

What I feel, need and want matters.

Additional Practice for Self-Expression

When you have time, please do yourself a favour and write letters to the people in your life, both past and present, towards whom you've never fully expressed yourself. Specifically, writing one letter to your mother and one to your father is extremely healing and liberating. Other significant people include: children, partners, spouses, ex-partners, siblings and friends. At first, please write each letter as though you're not going to give the letter to the person, so that you can be completely honest with yourself about your feelings without holding anything back. Please keep in mind that it's okay, and also healthy, to express your anger as you write, because it's better to get this energy out than to keep it in. Later on, if you'd like actually to send/give a letter to any or all of these important people, you can write a less reactive version. If there are people in your life who have passed away whom you (1) never found closure with or (2) simply want to share things with, please also write them a letter.

CHAPTER 9

Surrender Now and Let Go

When you surrender to what is and so become fully present, the past ceases to have any power. The realm of Being, which had been obscured by the mind, then opens up. Suddenly, a great stillness arises within you, an unfathomable sense of peace. And within that peace, there is great joy. And within that joy, there is love. And at the innermost core, there is the sacred, the immeasurable, That which cannot be named.

Eckhart Tolle

Wherever you are, please take a few slow, deep breaths into your belly. Feel your whole body, from your feet all the way up to the crown of your head, and then down to your fingertips. Please relax any tension you feel and let yourself be. Using each inhalation to open your body and create inner space, welcome everything you're thinking, feeling and experiencing here in this moment. Please be present to your body and your breath.

Most of our suffering and unhappiness arises when we fight what we're thinking, feeling or experiencing in the present moment. This is why most of our healing and happiness are found through accepting whatever is going on within us and around us in the here and now. When we stop running from the truth we fear, we immediately empower ourselves to see the thoughts, beliefs, emotions, habits and situations that are not grounded in a deep love and respect for ourselves, ultimately so we can transform and heal these aspects of our lives. This is why learning to stop, let go and open fully to life in the present moment is key to identifying everything we're unconsciously allowing to limit us or hold us back.

If we want to be happy and enjoy our lives, we're called to let go of our resistance to everything we're not at peace, happy or satisfied with, because it's only through complete inner acceptance of these things that we can truly redirect our thoughts, words and actions towards creating what we want and need. Beneath our internal battle with anyone or anything, we'll always find our fears of losing control, of losing our identity, of losing love, and ultimately of experiencing the unprocessed emotional pain that we've internalized in the past. In other words, underneath everything and everyone that we're reactive towards and feel somehow restricts our inner freedom, peace or happiness, we're once again just protecting ourselves from feeling uncomfortable, scary or overwhelming emotions.

Ironically, the parts of our lives that challenge us the most always represent the things we're most attached to and are thus afraid of living without. In fact, whatever or whomever we grasp onto, to our own detriment, clearly shows us where we're still not fully accepting, valuing or trusting ourselves. Internally, we become attached to limiting beliefs about ourselves and the world because they protect us and distract us from facing what we fear feeling. The same is also true of our self-destructive patterns of behaviour and our addictions. Beneath all of our habitual reactions, obsessions and compulsions, all that exists are painful emotions that we haven't felt safe or supported to express or process openly. Externally, we become attached to people, situations, jobs, money and material possessions for the very same reasons. Underneath our attachments in the outer world, we always find the same fears of losing control, of losing our identity, of losing love and, ultimately, of facing the uncomfortable emotions that we've denied and suppressed throughout our lives.

Thankfully, all of our attachments are connected to internal reactions that are purposefully designed first to protect us and then later to guide us towards total freedom. Our attachments, and the fear and insecurity beneath them, actually show us exactly where we must surrender in our daily lives so we can let go of whatever or whomever we're still allowing to hold us back or drain our vital life-force energy, health and happiness.

If you realize that all things change, there is nothing
you will try to hold on to. If you are not afraid of dying,
there is nothing you cannot achieve.

Lao Tzu

To surrender fully we're called to let go of our compulsive need to control ourselves, other people and our environments, which means we must break through our fears of feeling vulnerable. Underneath our lack of openness, acceptance and trust, we often don't want to acknowledge how we really feel, or we don't want others to see all of who we are, especially what we do not love about ourselves. Ultimately, there is nothing that we're not capable of transforming or re-creating, so when we love ourselves enough finally to surrender our inner fight and accept the truth, we find that the love inside of us is strong enough to heal anything that has been painful or scary for us. Regardless of how long we avoid addressing a particular issue, the time will always come when we cannot run from it any longer. At these points in our personal growth, whether it comes about in a healthy way or in a destructive way, we have to stop denying what we feel and finally accept the fact that we can only change our own approach to ourselves and to life. When these times inevitably arise, we're called to stop trying to control the outside world and to stop our attempts to change other people. Through this inner pressure, life is asking us to follow our heart towards the activities, situations and relationships that support us to feel alive and well. Rather than continuing to abandon our feelings based on a self-destructive desire to maintain control or avoid the implications of the truth, we're being challenged to break through our self-imposed limitations and finally to give ourselves permission to let go, enjoy the unknown and be happy now.

> *God, grant me the serenity to accept the things I cannot change, the courage to change the things I can, and the wisdom to know the difference.*
>
> **Reinhold Niebuhr**

If we look to the natural world, we see that it organically releases whatever limits its greatest potential for vitality and life. In the same way that many trees naturally let go of their leaves each autumn to make room for new growth and fresh life, we too are meant to release the parts of ourselves, our lives and our past that no longer serve our evolution and enjoyment of life. Since we are integral parts of nature, when we finally value ourselves and surrender to our inner truth completely we begin to want to let go of anything or anyone that we've allowed to limit us or hold us back. As we learn to love ourselves, we stop allowing ourselves to settle for sickness, misery or unhealthy compromise, and this unfolding dynamic always entails letting go of the beliefs, habits, cold comforts and situations that no longer reflect our true self or life purpose. Just like the tree that is destined simply to be itself and to grow into a full expression of who it truly is, we too are destined to respect ourselves enough to live our lives as a full expression of who we truly are.

> *When I let go of what I am, I become what I might be.*
> *When I let go of what I have, I receive what I need.*
>
> **Lao Tzu**

Letting go of close relationships is often one of our greatest lessons and challenges. It is never easy to let go of someone you truly love. And change is often harder than we want to admit. Whether it's death, divorce or another form of separation, trying to move on brings grief and sadness for the joy and connection that's passed. Or for the unresolved hurt and misunderstanding we've felt. But we would not be on the edge of release if it were not meant to be for our highest good. Sometimes we outgrow a relationship. Sometimes a person outgrows us. Sometimes it's just someone's time to go. Either way, we are forced to befriend the parts of us we have abandoned, rejected or denied in exchange for love, comfort or companionship. We are challenged to step into the unknown and to trust this is as it is meant to be.

We are all asked by life, the universe and God to come home to ourselves eventually, whether it's through the death of a relationship or in our physical death. So holding on to someone who limits us or feels limited by us really only causes pain. Eventually we have to face our underlying fears and insecurities if we truly want to be healthy, happy and free. In my personal life as well as my professional work, I have found that there is only one effective approach to letting go of situations and relationships that are not optimal for us any longer. This often-forgotten key entails becoming clear about what we actually want in life now, expressing it to the universe or God, and moving towards it, while focusing our time and energy on what makes us feel good, alive and well each day. We have to train ourselves to choose activities and relationships we can fully be ourselves in, as opposed to ones where we feel compromised or obliged to please.

As you become more accustomed to focusing on things that make you feel good daily, you will naturally move away from anyone or anything that is not healthy for you. Those people who are meant to be with you on your destined path will organically come with you, while those who limit you, do not meet you or do not value you, will naturally be left behind. Through this process, every unresolved emotion, limiting belief or incomplete situation that needs to be transformed will naturally surface to be addressed when the time is right. Our only task becomes feeling everything that's present, regardless of how painful or scary, and then making a conscious choice to speak and act honestly, kindly and respectfully based on our heart's truth and instinct now.

When guilt arises, it's an opportunity to address it consciously and see how often it holds us back from being authentic and true to ourselves. Since you're the only person who can allow yourself to live fully before your time comes to leave your body in this lifetime, only you can give yourself permission to let go of guilt and enjoy your life, even if other people close to you are still struggling in some way. Knowing this, are you finally ready to stop making yourself wrong for wanting to be happy, and to accept that it's okay to enjoy your precious days before you're forced to let go of everything and everyone?

Practical Questions

In which situations and relationships do you find yourself constantly reacting?

Which people and environments do you struggle with and thus avoid?

Can you try to remain centred, present and non-reactive in these situations by breathing slowly and deeply?

Who or what are you attached to and do you intuitively know is holding you back?

Why are you afraid of moving on and letting this person, situation or thing go?

Who in your life do you try to control? Your partner or spouse? Your children or parents? Are you afraid that they will abandon you or hurt you if you allow them to do as they please? Why are you afraid?

Who in your life do you feel controlled or dominated by? Are you afraid of losing their love, upsetting them or being abandoned by them? Why are you afraid?

Are you attached to your material possessions? Are you afraid of losing any material object that you 'own'? If so, why?

Do you identify with your material possessions?

Do you think they define who you are?

Can you name any belief or story you tell yourself that you know limits you and holds you back in life?

Key Affirmations

I am willing to let go of my need to control life.

All control is an illusion.

I am willing to surrender my inner fight. I have suffered enough.

It's okay for me to let go and find peace.

It's okay for me to slow down and stop. I do not need to be busy all the time.

My possessions cannot, do not and will never define me.

I face my fears and move forward anyway.

I am okay, and I will be okay.

I am one with life. Everything is as it's meant to be for my healing and growth.

[Your name], let go, let go, let go.

CHAPTER 10

Deep Self-Respect

When you think everything is someone else's fault, you will suffer a lot. When you realize that everything springs only from yourself, you will learn both peace and joy.

His Holiness the 14th Dalai Lama

Wherever you are, please take a few slow, deep breaths into your belly. Feel your whole body, from your feet all the way up to the crown of your head, and then down to your fingertips. Please relax any tension you feel and let yourself be. Using each inhalation to open your body and create inner space, welcome everything you're thinking, feeling and experiencing here in this moment. Please be present to your body and your breath.

I have learned that we're given a choice in life between feeling sorry for ourselves and respecting ourselves. But we cannot have both. I think it's safe to presume that all of us would choose dignity over victimhood or self-pity if we knew how. Most of us never learn that by blaming other people or circumstances outside of ourselves for how we feel or for the life we've created, we are literally giving away our personal power to find deep peace, happiness and true love. If we sincerely want to free ourselves from suffering and to create a fulfilling life that we enjoy, each of us is called to accept one hundred per cent responsibility for our lives in their entirety.

If you're aware that you place blame outside of yourself for any reason, or that you play the victim sometimes with certain people, or in certain situations, please know that you're not alone. We all do it. All of us have played, or still play, the victim at times in our lives because it is the most common way we've all learned to get what we want and need, both from life and from other people. If you imagine a small child who cries, throws a tantrum or pouts to get their parents' attention, or to get what they want and need, you have a perfect example of what I mean. Now please consider – and please open your mind to accepting the fact – that this same small child is most likely still alive inside of you, leading you to react and play the victim in your life, along with almost everyone else on our planet, including myself.

If we're honest with ourselves, we see how at times we complain about or blame people and factors outside of ourselves for the hurt, unhappiness and dissatisfaction we feel in relation to our current life circumstances. This victim consciousness that so many of us live in is one of the most self-destructive and self-sabotaging belief patterns we need to transform in order to respect ourselves and be happy. The 'poor me' way of life that so many of us are trapped in, to some degree ultimately keeps us stuck in the very situations and relationships in which we feel hurt and victimized. If we truly want to find lasting peace, we must stop allowing ourselves to believe that we are, or ever have been, the victim in any way, in any situation or relationship. The sensitive truth is that at a very young age most of us learned that if we played the victim, expressed hurt or blamed other people, we could get what we wanted and needed from them, particularly our parents. To survive, all of us learned that by making other people feel wrong, bad, guilty or sorry for us, we could manipulate our world and thus receive the energy, love, attention and support we needed at a given point in our growth and evolution. We simply didn't know better.

But now, as of this moment, we do. And once we're aware of this dynamic, we can never truly go back – especially if we want to be well or fulfil our life's purpose. In every moment of every day, we're either unconsciously channelling our energy towards blaming other people and circumstances outside of ourselves or we're consciously channelling our energy towards creating a healthy, happy and fulfilling life. If we truly want to be content both personally and professionally, we have to stop blaming other people, factors and circumstances outside of ourselves for how we feel or for where we are in our lives. Whether it feels like a heavenly dream or a hell-like nightmare, our lives are, and will always be, completely our own creations.

Even in situations where we've experienced abuse, whether physical, sexual or verbal, it's crucial that we eventually 'find the light' by looking for the purpose or lesson that the trauma or pain served. In certain circumstances this can indeed be difficult; however, at some point, it's in our own best interest to stop blaming others as well as ourselves so we can move forward and truly be happy. To achieve this, we're called to rise above all forms of blame and to expand our perception on the meaning of our life experiences so we can finally stick up for, honour and respect ourselves now in the ways we haven't always known how to. Regardless of how powerless we may have felt in the past, we're all challenged to heal the pain and anger present within us now so that we can exercise forgiveness and compassion for everyone involved and then move forward freely, empowered, and much more aware.

As the old cliché tells us – *if it doesn't kill you it only makes you stronger* – every life experience, regardless of how painful, scary or seemingly 'wrong' it was, introduces us to our inherent strength and our unlimited capacity to overcome any obstacle we face. We cannot change what's happened in the past, but we can change how much we allow it to stop us from being happy and well. This doesn't make behaviour like physical or sexual abuse okay, but using past injustices as a reason not to create the best life possible now is not healthy for anyone. Both personally and professionally I've witnessed people who've endured the most extreme abuses imaginable reclaim their health and happiness by accepting their wounds as important experiences that served them in fulfilling their life's larger purpose to bring unconditional love, compassion, forgiveness and wisdom into our world.

No one saves us but ourselves. No one can and no one may.
We ourselves must walk the path.

Buddha

We can never truly love and respect ourselves when we're blaming other people or external circumstances for any reason, because it's impossible to feel good about ourselves when we perceive ourselves to be a victim. When we blame we actually give our personal power, energy and happiness away to whomever or whatever we're trying to project responsibility on to. If we keep blaming, even in the smallest of ways, we unconsciously commit to remain trapped in the very situations, memories and self-destructive patterns that we actually want freedom from.

The simple truth is we can only find healing, happiness and self-respect to the degree we're willing to be accountable for our lives. Eventually we have to acknowledge that our lives, as they manifest in the outside world, are simply the product of our own beliefs, thoughts, emotions, actions and spoken words. Our lives are ultimately just the accumulated result of all the beliefs we've ever held, all the thoughts we've ever thought, all the emotions we've ever felt, all the actions we've ever taken, and all the words we've ever spoken in all of the past moments leading up to this one. Likewise, the life we experience from this moment onwards is also entirely our own creation. The beliefs, thoughts, emotions, actions and spoken words alive within us right now, which we're expressing out into the world, are the energy and vibration with which we're both creating and attracting all of our coming life experiences.

The only way to transform the wounds that continue to surface as a result of the disrespect that we allow or put up with is to accept full responsibility for the parts of our lives we've unintentionally created. This is done by speaking and acting honestly now, which means we're finally valuing what we feel, need and want rather than self-destructively trying to get someone to please us or save us. By making the choice to be true to ourselves daily and thus focusing on what makes us feel alive and well, we stop betraying ourselves or allowing ourselves to be mistreated, which is how we prevent feelings of self-loathing and self-pity from destroying our lives.

I do not believe in a fate that falls on men however they act;
but I do believe in a fate that falls on them unless they act.

Buddha

Ironically, the people we tend to blame or feel victimized around always represent the relationships in which we betray and hurt ourselves in some way. Once we finally realize how self-destructive it is when we do not value and express ourselves in every situation, we can finally take responsibility for our own health and happiness by being true to ourselves no matter what. No one wants to waste their precious days attacking others or sitting in self-pity, which is why we all need to understand that we're only ever the victim of our fears. So, when fear arises we can still choose to be authentic and not waste our time and energy reactively blaming other people or feeling sorry for ourselves. We can teach ourselves to break through our unconscious patterns of manipulation and get clear about honouring what we love, want and need now to move forward.

Through this process we stop expecting other people to make us happy, and we realize that much of the disappointment we feel towards others is really self-created disappointment that results from never learning how to make ourselves happy. We all learn to neglect ourselves to please others, thinking this will bring us happiness and love. In return we expect others to behave in ways that please us too, and when they do not, we experience hurt or anger, but this hurt and anger is really caused by our fears or the gap in our emotional awareness, which is what leads us to reject and harm ourselves.

As we deepen our self-awareness and thus become mindful when we're sabotaging ourselves in this way, we become much quicker to reclaim our energy from the people and circumstances we blame, feel victim to or expect to make us happy. Eventually we realize that reactive tantrums, behaving aggressively, hoping others will please us or trying to make other people feel bad will never actually get us what we want. When we stop blaming external forces for the life we've created and thus take responsibility for everything we think, feel, do and say, we finally start to feel good about the person we see looking back at us in the mirror each day. By speaking and acting with kindness and honesty now, even if we're scared, hurt or unclear, we stop creating so much discomfort and shame for ourselves, and this finally brings us the deep peace and self-respect we're looking for.

Practical Questions

In which situations and relationships do you feel like
a victim right now?

Where and with whom in the past have you felt like a victim?

Who and what do you blame for where you are in life or for what
you're doing in your life right now?

Who and what do you constantly complain about? What can you
do to change your approach to the situation or person now?

Do you still blame your parents, your partner, your spouse,
your children, God or anyone else for any reason?

Who do you expect to save you, rescue you, take care of
you or make you happy?

Who do you try to save, rescue, take care of or make happy?

If you've ever experienced physical or sexual abuse,
either as a child or adult, can you see how the trauma may
have taught you the importance of (1) sticking up for yourself,
(2) expressing your feelings, (3) overcoming fear, (4) forgiving
yourself, and (5) forgiving others?

Once again, where and with who in your life are you betraying
or hurting yourself?

How are you allowing fear to make you a victim currently?

Key Affirmations

I am not a victim. I never have been and I never will be.

I am one hundred per cent responsible for my life and for everything I experience.

I am one hundred per cent responsible for the life I have created.

I am one hundred per cent responsible for the life I experience from today onwards.

I will not blame anyone or anything ever again. I will not give my power away.

I don't need to get sick to be loved, appreciated or recognized.

I have everything I need within me to create a fulfilling life that I love.

I cannot save or rescue anyone. They must heal and fulfil themselves.

No one can save me or rescue me. I must heal and fulfil myself.

I am ready to stop blaming myself. It's okay to move on, forgive and be happy.

I chose everything in my life in order to fulfil my life's purpose.

CHAPTER 11

Love and Heal Your Inner Child

In every real man a child is hidden that wants to play.

Friedrich Nietzsche

Wherever you are, please take a few slow, deep breaths into your belly. Feel your whole body, from your feet all the way up to the crown of your head, and then down to your fingertips. Please relax any tension you feel and let yourself be. Using each inhalation to open your body and create inner space, welcome everything you're thinking, feeling and experiencing here in this moment. Please be present to your body and your breath.

The term 'wounded inner child' typically refers to the emotional pain experienced during childhood that currently remains unhealed within us. The reason it's optimal to address this topic at this stage in the book is because our psychological and emotional wounds from childhood are directly connected to the situations and relationships that are currently full of victimhood and blame. In order to love and heal ourselves fully, we subconsciously create experiences in the present that mirror experiences from our past, often from childhood, so we can (1) transform the associated pain that is still stored within us and (2) learn the important lessons necessary to fulfil our life's purpose and awaken spiritually. If we have not fully healed a past experience or period that was painful or confusing, then we will instinctually create situations in the present that reflect back to us the unresolved emotions from the original incident(s), ultimately so we can make peace with our past, care for ourselves more deeply, and enjoy our life now.

The feelings of hurt and powerlessness that always co-arise with our patterns of blame and victimhood actually exist so that we can bring unconditional love and awareness to the child within us and heal these deeply rooted wounds from the past. Through giving ourselves the unconditional love that most of us did not receive as children, we can, in a sense, become the enlightened parents we never had, parent our own soul, and thus transform any limitations created during childhood. By using our innate intelligence to revisit past memories and experiences that were painful, scary, traumatic or love-deprived, we can fill these dark inner spaces with the love, compassion and belief in ourselves we've always needed to be happy and well.

Psychoanalysis is in essence a cure through love.

Sigmund Freud

Another way of looking at the process of healing our wounded inner child focuses primarily on the subtle relationship between our body and what we term our soul. Although our physical body and our soul are not actually separate in any way, from this particular perspective, when we encounter painful, scary or traumatic experiences as children, parts of us, or fragments of our soul, actually disassociate and leave our body until we feel it's safe to return. In these instances, the psychological and emotional pain is often too overwhelming for us to feel and process, so we repress both the emotion and the memory into some part of our physical body. This process literally pushes fragments of our soul out into the space surrounding our physical body (typically called our energy body). The overwhelming emotional pain often felt during childhood becomes bottled up in a way where it fills both the open spaces and the cells that make up our physical body, thereby forcing parts of our non-physical self outside our body until we're ready to heal these emotional wounds and embody these parts of our true self fully once again.

Each of us can heal our early emotional pain through creating a loving and safe environment within ourselves and our lives now. More specifically, we can go back both in time and in memory to invite all of ourselves, or all of our soul, back into our body by bringing the wisdom of our lived experience to our inner child. One of the best ways to achieve this is to open a dialogue between ourselves now and ourselves as a child, and the practices found at the end of this chapter will effectively guide you through this process. As you move forward, please keep in mind that healing our wounded inner child is a process that varies for each person. For some of us, this lifetime has been full of abuse and trauma, so it will take a little longer to reintegrate all of our soul back into our body and life. For others, this life has not been quite as traumatic, so the process of reintegrating all of our soul will not be as intensive. Either way, our innate intelligence already knows the best and most natural approach to our unique healing and personal awakening.

Our lives can be viewed simply as the journey from healing our wounded inner child to embodying an enlightened form of our inner child, because as we heal our repressed emotional pain and master the lessons we came here to learn, we not only rediscover the innocence, purity, openness and vulnerability of a child, but we also exemplify true wisdom, love, intelligence and self-awareness. Even if our childhood was extremely traumatic or painful, through giving ourselves the love we've always deserved, we can still liberate ourselves from our suffering and learn how to be happy now. The more loving attention we direct inwards towards healing our inner child, the sooner we welcome home the parts of ourselves that we've lost touch with and the more joyful, authentic and simple our lives become.

Writing a Letter *to* Your Inner Child

Step 1
Please find a quiet place where you feel safe to be
open and vulnerable.

Step 2
Please imagine yourself in the most beautiful place on earth.
What is the most beautiful place to you? Where is it?
What does it feel like to be there? Please visualize it, feel into it,
and connect to this place.

Step 3
Please imagine yourself sitting somewhere in this beautiful place,
and please imagine that your five-year-old self has now come to
sit with you.

Then, connecting to yourself at five years of age, please ask
yourself as the adult what you would tell your younger self if given
the chance. What did he or she need to know or hear at this age
but was never told? If you could go back in time and encourage
or affirm anything to your five-year-old self, what would you say?

Step 4
After taking some time to contemplate the questions above,
please write a letter to your five-year-old self. Please begin with
'Dear [your name]', and please express everything that you would
say to yourself as a five-year-old child if given the opportunity.
Then, take a few slow, deep breaths and allow yourself fully to
feel and experience whatever is true for you. Please notice any
memories that arise from the past.

Step 5
Repeat steps three and four while connecting with your
10-year-old self, your 15-year-old self, and your 20-year-old self.
Please feel free to do this with any additional age(s) if you feel
inspired to do so.

Writing a Letter *from* Your Inner Child

Step 1
Please find a quiet place where you feel safe to be open
and vulnerable.

Step 2
Please imagine yourself in the most beautiful place on earth.
What is the most beautiful place to you? Where is it?
What does it feel like to be there? Please visualize it,
feel into it, and connect to this place.

Step 3
Please imagine yourself sitting somewhere in this beautiful
place, and please imagine that your five-year-old self has now
come to sit with you.

Then, connecting to yourself at five years of age, please ask your
five-year-old self what he or she wants to tell you as the adult.
What does he or she want you to know or hear right now in your
life? What wisdom and healing does your five-year-old self need
to encourage in you as an adult right now?

Step 4
After taking some time to contemplate the questions above,
please write a letter from your five-year-old self addressed to
your adult self. Please begin with 'Dear [your name]', and express
everything that your five-year-old self wants you, the adult,
to know, hear and remember. Then, take a few slow, deep
breaths and allow yourself fully to feel and experience whatever
is true for you. Please notice any situations or relationships that
you're being guided to address in your life right now.

Key Affirmations

I am grateful for the important life lessons I learned
in my childhood.

My pain has made me strong and kind.

I forgive myself for not sticking up for myself in the past.

I forgive myself for compromising and abandoning
myself for love.

I am willing to forgive anyone who hurt, abused or mistreated me.

I forgive myself for any abuse or pain that I did not know
how to protect myself from.

I forgive myself and others for any abuse or pain that I witnessed.

It was not my fault. I am not to blame.

I am smart, capable, attractive, lovable, respectable and
secure in myself.

I am not a child any more. I will not allow my past to punish
me any longer.

I was born to enjoy a wonderful life.

I was born to have fun, to grow, to learn, to explore and to love.

Little [your name], I love you.

It's okay for me to have fun and joy in my life.

Additional Practice for Healing Your Inner Child

When you have some space, I recommend finding a picture, or pictures, of yourself as a child. Then, I recommend looking at the 'little you' in these pictures and expressing some of the affirmations listed above. For example, look at your younger self and say, '[Your name], I love you. You deserve to be loved just as you are. You are enough.' Please try this with as many photos as you like. This can be a very healing and liberating exercise if you allow it to be.

CHAPTER 12

Your Ego Is Not Your Enemy

There is a kind of experience so different from anything
the ego can offer that you will never want to cover
or hide it again ... The ego is afraid of the spirit's joy,
because once you have experienced it you will
withdraw all protection from the ego, and become
totally without investment in fear.

A Course in Miracles

Wherever you are, please take a few slow, deep breaths into your belly. Feel your whole body, from your feet all the way up to the crown of your head, and then down to your fingertips. Please relax any tension you feel and let yourself be. Using each inhalation to open your body and create inner space, welcome everything you're thinking, feeling and experiencing here in this moment. Please be present to your body and your breath.

Contrary to what most of us believe, our ego is not our enemy. In fact, if we make this part of our psyche wrong, we will stay trapped in suffering. I've found that we all create the cocoon of our ego as an act of unconditional self-love to protect us until we're ready to fully embody our true nature. The primary function of our ego is to protect our heart and soul in the same way that the cocoon protects the caterpillar throughout its metamorphosis into a butterfly. Our ego acts as our guardian until we're ready to break through our fears and live as a free and full expression of who we truly are each day.

The development of our ego is a natural part of our growth and evolution. In the same way that the caterpillar must create a cocoon to protect itself throughout its transformation into a butterfly, we too must develop our ego to protect us throughout our own transformation and awakening. Although the caterpillar is the creator of its cocoon, it is not the cocoon itself. Similarly, we are the creator of our ego, but we are not the ego itself. It is a nonphysical form of armour we construct mentally that we can outgrow if we're willing to take responsibility for doing so. Through loving ourselves unconditionally we can finally heal the mental, emotional and physical pain that our ego exists to protect us from. When we're sick or unhappy, our body and mind are actually asking us to let down the walls we created to survive before we knew how to value and be true to ourselves. If we want to find inner freedom and peace, each of us is called to open our mind to the larger reality beyond our defence mechanisms and our need to be right, better than or accepted by others.

To break free from the limitations of our ego as soon as possible, it's important to remember how and why we created this defensive aspect of our personality in the first place. Because the world didn't always feel very safe when we were growing up, we intuitively created a protective shell through which we could relate to both ourselves and to life. The overwhelming emotional and psychic energies that bombarded us as children were often too much for us to feel, process and understand on our own, and this drove all of us to create our ego to protect us from the painful and confusing energies that we encountered on a daily basis. In our desire to individuate from the world around us, each of us organically closed ourselves off and tried to separate ourselves from the outside world mentally, because instinctually we felt that doing so would give us some control over what was occurring. Out of what is an inherent love for ourselves, each of us built an all-encompassing psycho-energetic cocoon of perceived safety and security to protect our heart, knowing that one day we would finally cultivate the necessary awareness and skills to value our sensitivity and thus liberate ourselves. Since a very large number of us did not have people in our lives who had cultivated the awareness to lovingly mirror back to us what we were feeling as children, we never learned how to consciously express the thoughts and emotions that we were experiencing. Instead, many of us learned to reject, repress, deny, avoid and hide what we felt and thought in order to survive, which then gave birth to hurt, anger, shame and the defensive aspects of our personality.

The degree to which our ego initially developed depended upon the amount of protection we intuitively felt we needed as children. Thus the strength and thickness of this protective layer of our personality varies for each of us depending on how painful and confusing our lives have been. If the family and larger environments that we grew up in did not support us to honour, process and be present to what we felt on a daily basis (and most did not), we will have built up a much stronger ego and disconnected from our emotions to a larger degree. This is a natural response to not knowing how to attend to our feelings for ourselves. If, on the other hand, we grew up with emotionally aware and present parents, then we would have been supported in understanding and expressing our emotions and would not have needed to build up such strong walls.

As we age, most of us just remain trapped in our protective cocoon – especially those of us with big egos – because we never learn how to heal our unresolved emotional pain. The safe and familiar confines often become comfortable, simply because we fear facing the emotions that are stored in our body and subconscious mind. If we don't wake up and reconnect with our true feelings, needs and dreams by the time we reach all the responsibilities of 'adulthood', often we continue living our lives disconnected from our soul and completely identify with a small illusion about who we are. An alarmingly large number of us end up settling for a limited existence, because liberating ourselves would entail feeling all of the love as well as all of the fear we've denied for so long. To the majority of us, it simply appears easier to continue living in cold comfort, hiding out in the familiarity of our protected world. Having lived with our hearts closed to our true self for so long, we've mistakenly come to identify with the limiting voice of our ego rather than the expansive soul that's been waiting to break free. Slowing down, becoming vulnerable, and breaking the habits that keep us safe can be hard to do after so many years of being disconnected and cold.

> *Enter by the narrow gate; for wide is the gate and broad is the way that leads to destruction, and there are many who go in by it. Because narrow is the gate and difficult is the way which leads to life, and there are few who find it.*
>
> **Matthew 7:13–14**

Our ego-based thinking keeps us reacting to life, constantly running from our heart in the present moment to protect us from being vulnerable. The thoughts that just don't stop coming are merely symptoms of undigested emotions and experiences that our ego is currently guarding. We've also developed such a strong momentum of habitual thinking to run away from any truth or pain that we fear. This protective aspect of our personality very skilfully avoids whatever is uncomfortable internally and externally by constantly manufacturing thoughts about the past and the future to prevent us from feeling overwhelmed, insecure or out of control in the present. As a result of this dynamic, many of us remain trapped in our head, stuck reacting to life in ways that stop us from finding the inner peace, health and happiness we desire. We're not aware of it, but in constantly denying any truth related to our psychological, emotional and physical pain, we not only create more sickness and misery, but we also cover up the abundant source of love within us that is intended to heal, fulfil and sustain each of us.

In avoiding the mental and emotional discomfort that we've internalized and disconnected from over the years, we start compounding the suffering that we were initially trying to avoid. In this way, our ego's purposeful protection, which is necessary to a point, eventually begins to create additional pain on top of the suffering it was originally created to shelter us from. When we constantly numb ourselves to our inner struggles, we not only avoid healing them, but we also avoid understanding their root cause. Another analogy that demonstrates the purpose and function of our ego quite well is that of using painkillers to relieve physical pain. In the same way that we might take a painkiller to relieve ourselves from feeling the pain of a backache, our ego relieves us from feeling pain that is hard for us to handle at particular points in time. In taking a painkiller to remedy back pain, the underlying conditions that caused the back pain are still present; we've just numbed ourselves to them. We experience temporary relief and believe that our pain has gone away, but in reality the pain and its source remain unhealed.

Our ego's protective function is very similar. Our ego temporarily covers our pain so that we can function and carry on in our lives. However, just like a painkiller, the relief our ego brings is only short term, because the pain and its source still remain unhealed. The same pain that was briefly masked will surface again and again until we understand its underlying cause, heal it, and therefore liberate ourselves from it for good. From this perspective, if we have chronic back pain and we continue taking painkillers on a regular basis without looking deeper into the source of the pain, besides developing an immunity to the painkilling function and thus needing higher doses, we'll also begin building up toxicity in our body from all the chemicals in the painkillers. In situations like this, we live unaware of our affliction's root cause and the affliction itself remains unhealed. Our approach to managing our pain, which initially seemed supportive and loving, eventually just becomes a further source of suffering.

Seen in this light, the same can be said for our ego. We all unconsciously create our ego in order to protect us. But eventually we create additional suffering for ourselves because in continuously disconnecting from our pain, we not only avoid healing it; we also avoid addressing its source. Our initial way of managing our psychological and emotional struggles, which once provided temporary effective relief, just creates more misery and sickness in our lives when we do not transform the underlying issues. This dynamic pushes away people we love, positive opportunities, and renders our heart closed to receiving the very things we're asking for.

For most of us it's not until our suffering becomes so intense and compounded that our protective shell cracks and we open to approaching life from new perspectives. We tend to be so stubborn and closed-minded because in the past we've felt the need to fight just to survive. But now, to bring down the walls, life has to get really difficult before we'll finally surrender and change our thinking, views or lifestyle habits. Quite often it's not until we're somehow forced to face our fears through a breakdown or serious wake-up call, that we finally open our heart to feeling our way through life and healing the protective aspects of our personality that we're destined to outgrow. Whether the catalyst is a physical illness, a new intimate relationship, the breakdown of a longstanding relationship, the death of a loved one, a suicidal depression, a newborn child, financial hardship or an important goal, the point always comes in our growth where our ego becomes limiting and unhealthy. When this time inevitably arrives, we're all given an opportunity to be vulnerable, address the truth, and release the unconscious need for control and separation that is no longer serving us.

The creation of our ego is indeed a necessary and purposeful part of our soul's evolutionary unfolding, because we must create what we perceive to be a separate self in order to fulfil our life's purpose and master loving ourselves unconditionally. All of us must protect ourselves until we're ready to liberate ourselves from all self-imposed limitations. However, just as the creation of our ego is a necessary step in both remembering who we are and learning to love ourselves, so too is our eventual liberation from it. As we grow in awareness we're naturally guided from within to break through our fear-based defence mechanisms so that we can heal all the uncomfortable emotions that we've repressed throughout our lives. Since we all want to love and be loved, eventually we realize our walls need to come down for us to be happy. We have to overcome our fears of letting others in or of allowing people to see our darkness and our light. If we're always scared of connecting intimately and deeply, then we just keep hiding behind a mask, pretending to be someone we're not, feeling alone and misunderstood. Likewise, if we continue to make the aspects of ourselves associated with our ego wrong, this subtle self-judgement, criticism and rejection will only keep us trapped and stuck. Thankfully, once we're prepared to accept our ego completely, while speaking and acting from our true feelings, it becomes much easier to finally just be ourselves and enjoy our life.

CHAPTER 13

Understand Your Life Purpose

When I was five years old, my mother always told me that happiness was the key to life. When I went to school, they asked me what I wanted to be when I grew up. I wrote down 'happy'. They told me I didn't understand the assignment, and I told them they didn't understand life.

John Lennon

Wherever you are, please take a few slow, deep breaths into your belly. Feel your whole body, from your feet all the way up to the crown of your head, and then down to your fingertips. Please relax any tension you feel and let yourself be. Using each inhalation to open your body and create inner space, welcome everything you're thinking, feeling and experiencing here in this moment. Please be present to your body and your breath.

The questions 'Why am I here?' and 'What is my life purpose?' are at the heart of every human life. If we truly want to be happy, well and at peace, we're called to remember, with crystal clarity, why we were born. Understanding that your life has a purpose and that all suffering is purposeful can help you find the strength to persist with your healing and spiritual journey when you're struggling. As with the destiny of every human being, your destiny entails learning how to love, value and be true to yourself completely, which then unlocks the love within you and allows you simply to enjoy being alive.

It's helpful to know that our choices, spoken words and actions in each moment are either leading us closer to fulfilling our life's purpose or creating more pain, misery and sickness. Every experience that we've had since our birth right up until this very moment has been teaching us to accept, forgive, honour, value, respect, express, trust in and be true to ourselves so that we can know the clarity and bliss that are inherent to our true nature, and then bring loving-kindness into the world. Although it may seem impractical or even blasphemous to assert, I've found that a very large part of our purpose in life also involves remembering that what we tend to call our 'self', our 'soul' or our 'spirit' is actually God manifesting in a unique form through what we perceive as our physical and non-physical being. From this perspective, each of us is a unique expression of atomic energy and universal intelligence in human form. You and I, as well as every other person alive – regardless of skin colour, religious belief, economic status and cultural background – are destined to live a fully awakened life where we understand the miracle of our existence as well as our unity with nature, other human beings and the larger universe. Whether or not we choose to align with this aspect of our purpose is entirely up to us as individuals, but the fact remains that we're here to break through every self-imposed limitation, false belief and form of suffering, so that we can be ourselves and enjoy our life.

I searched for God, and found only myself. I searched for myself, and found only God.

Sufi proverb

Even though all of us begin our quest for true happiness, purpose and love by looking outside of ourselves, eventually we realize that no external person, situation or relationship can truly give us the answers we're looking for. There will always come a time when we're forced to accept that it's only through looking within ourselves, through following the subtle whispers of our own heart and soul, and through trusting our own innate intelligence, that we can find the clarity and sense of knowing we're seeking. The universal intelligence that expresses in, as, and through each of us is always guiding us forward towards our most fulfilling life. So once we're wholeheartedly committed to being true to ourselves daily, we can surrender into the natural force and flow of life itself, which then leads us directly, and as effortlessly as possible, towards everything that we truly want and need.

Your work is to discover your work and then with all your heart to give yourself to it.

Buddha

Eventually we come to understand that we're all pioneers in our own lives, because no one has ever, can ever or will ever walk in our shoes. Our unique path through life is uncharted territory, which means our personal destiny and awakening are unfolding in a way that is particular to our own karma, purpose and inner learning. In each moment and with each breath we're all actually charting our own distinct course towards bringing the love that we are fully into this world. As we go through the inner healing and strengthening necessary to value ourselves in every moment and relationship, the unique gifts and talents that we were born to share organically surface, essentially so that we can create our lives based upon these deep inner truths. On a very personal level, beyond knowing the importance of creating a healthy relationship with yourself that is based on unconditional love, kindness, respect and compassion, *no one can tell you exactly how* to go about fulfilling your life's purpose. We all have to listen to the subtle inner voice of our heart and soul and learn to follow this guidance into and through our deepest fears, doubts and insecurities.

Over time, our choices and actions become driven less by external motivations or conditioning and more by the inner call of our soul, which is always guiding us towards more happiness, love and truth. By honouring what we feel, we naturally come to know, without doubt or confusion, who we are and why we came here. Eventually our heart opens enough to remember that only love matters, and this is when we start to release the aspects of our lives that are not grounded in deep self-worth and respect because we finally admit that these situations do not support our health, happiness or capacity to give back to life. In due time, it becomes clear that our life experiences are simply lessons supporting us to enjoy life as we learn to love ourselves, others and life wholeheartedly.

At the centre of your being you have the answer;
you know who you are and you know what you want.

Lao Tzu

After looking for my own purpose desperately, I found some very simple truths that have been both liberating and empowering to understand. Because I want you to find what you're looking for as soon as possible, it is helpful to know that your purpose entails:

1. Enjoying each day as much as possible in healthy ways, rather than self-destructive ones.
2. Learning to love yourself unconditionally in every moment and relationship, which primarily means speaking and acting based on what you truly feel in every situation, with kindness, mindfulness and mutual respect.
3. You also have to purge or heal all the emotions stored in your body from the past; like guilt, insecurity, fear, shame, anger, hurt and sadness.

4. To love others, to give love and to enjoy love, through relationships, being alone with nature, with animals, and through whatever work you're engaged in.

5. To create whatever you feel like from the love, truth and inspiration you feel, whether this is art, a home, a business, a family, cooking or events. Here there is no right or wrong. No good or bad. No better than or less than. It's simply what you want and what makes you come alive.

6. When it comes to merging the above purpose(s) with work and making a living, if you honour the above points, and simply do what feels the best, the most authentic, and the most full of life each day, then you will only say yes to jobs/a career/work that are aligned with who you really are and how you truly feel.

We try to plan everything from the mind, which gets us in trouble. We try to choose a vocation from the level of thought and map our entire life, which only leads to unhappiness and boredom. Not following our heart is how we try to maintain the illusion of control, which is really how we protect ourselves from the pain we associate with rejection, failure, judgement or losing pride. If we want to be happy and feel as though our work and life have both purpose and meaning, then we have to follow our heart each day. Through doing so, we can make this practical enough to support our material, physical or financial needs, and we can also harness the energy of our passion to become completely financially free.

We all look for our purpose 'out there' in the world, because we never learned that we ourselves are our purpose. Valuing the miracle of our life, freeing ourselves from suffering, and connecting with the people we love, is very

The true or primary purpose of your life cannot be found on the outer level. It does not concern what you do but what you are – that is to say, your state of consciousness ... Your inner purpose is to awaken ... It is that simple. You share that purpose with every other person on the planet – because it is the purpose of humanity. Your inner purpose is an essential part of the purpose of the whole, the universe and its emerging intelligence ... Finding and living in alignment with the inner purpose is the foundation for fulfilling your outer purpose. It is the basis for true success. Without that alignment, you can still achieve certain things through effort, struggle, determination, and sheer hard work or cunning. But there is no joy in such endeavour, and it invariably ends in some form of suffering.

Eckhart Tolle

much why we were born. Enjoying what makes us happy or feel well, while both respecting and caring for our body and our heart, is how we feel we matter and see the purpose of being alive. Having love for ourselves, love for the work we do, and love in the relationships we engage in each day, is what makes life truly worth living.

We live during a time when many people value money, university degrees, material possessions, social acceptance, the illusion of social status, and media attention over and above love, truth, kindness, meaning, peace and authentic connection. So it's easy to lose yourself in the unhealthy beliefs and drives of society, the media, your parents or your peers. If you don't let fear guide your decisions or stop you from being true to your heart, and you take good care of your health, then you will always have what you need to survive, and you will also find everything you need to thrive.

Practical Questions

Are you happy and satisfied with the work you do on a daily basis? If not, why not?

If you could do something that you love and are passionate about each day and also support yourself financially doing it, what would you choose to do?

Who or what are you allowing to stop you from focusing on your passions each day?

What fears are holding you back?

Are material comfort and money more important than your health and happiness?

Why are you here on earth?

Can you remember what you dreamed of doing and being as a child? Can you recall your sacred mission or soul contract in this lifetime?

Are you waiting for your children to age, your parents to die, or your intimate relationship to end before you start honouring your true needs and desires? If so, why?

If you only had one year to live, what would you change?
What would you go and do, experience or accomplish?
Who would you forgive? Who would you reach out to?
Who would you express yourself to fully?

Key Affirmations

It's okay to be happy.

It's okay to enjoy my life and my work each day.

I am destined to create a fulfilling life that I love.

I have everything I need to fulfil my life's purpose and liberate my soul.

I am pure, unconditional love.

I am exactly where I need to be to master loving myself.

I was not born to suffer. I am here to love, and to enjoy my life.

I give myself permission to be honest, happy and well.

I now give myself permission to do what I love daily.

CHAPTER 14

At Home In Yourself

One must learn to love oneself with a wholesome and healthy love, so that one can bear to be with oneself and need not roam.

Friedrich Nietzsche

Wherever you are, please take a few slow, deep breaths into your belly. Feel your whole body, from your feet all the way up to the crown of your head, and then down to your fingertips. Please relax any tension you feel and let yourself be. Using each inhalation to open your body and create inner space, welcome everything you're thinking, feeling and experiencing here in this moment. Please be present to your body and your breath.

Deep down, we all want to feel 'welcome', that we 'belong', and that we're accepted just the way we are. We also want to feel appreciated, simply because we're alive and not just for how we please others. Essentially, each of us holds a longing to feel at home within ourselves, because when we feel safe to simply be ourselves, where no one is judging us, and we can let our guard down to be vulnerable, our heart opens and allows the peace, joy and love within us to flow freely. To feel the warm embrace of unconditional love that most of us associate with the idea of 'home' is how we as human beings come to blossom and thrive. Even if our own experiences at home, either as children or as adults, have never been as loving or as warm as we've wanted them to be, deep down we all know it's possible to live in supportive environments that are full of kindness, respect, acceptance, understanding and joy.

For various reasons, many of us still have not found, or created, the home we're looking for. What we're rarely taught, and often don't realize, is that the one true home that we're all intuitively pursuing already exists within us just below the inner battles that we're subconsciously doing everything in our power to avoid. The only reason why any of us do not feel at home within ourselves and therefore within our lives is simply because we're reacting to and trying to escape the repressed emotions that still remain unresolved within us. More specifically, most of us are currently running from life itself in the here and now, because we fear facing the aspects of ourselves, our lives, and our past that we have not fully accepted, forgiven or learned to love unconditionally yet.

Regardless of what coming home, going home or being at home means to each of us as unique individuals, the home we're all looking for can never truly be found outside of ourselves. We can create loving and warm environments in the outer world, but doing so is always dependent on, and reflective of, how loving and warm we feel within and towards ourselves. Sometimes we may think we've found our home in another person or a specific place, but if we do not wholeheartedly love, value and accept ourselves, then eventually the fact that we are not at peace within ourselves will always resurface to be addressed. This is why coming home to life in the present moment, moment after moment, day after day, is one of the most important keys to loving ourselves unconditionally, transforming our suffering and finally enjoying our lives.

Although we may think there was, or will be, a more opportune time, we cannot love ourselves or liberate our soul in some long-gone past or in some distant fantasy of the future. We can only love and therefore heal and free ourselves right here in this very moment by creating a loving, safe environment within our own body, heart and mind. Initially it may seem impractical to become this focused on the present moment, but eventually it becomes clear that a significant amount of our life, time, energy and money are wasted on thinking about the future and the past.

*The secret of health for both mind and body is not to mourn
for the past, worry about the future, or anticipate troubles,
but to live in the present moment wisely and earnestly.*

Buddha

Through consistently living with our awareness focused
on what is true in this moment, we empower ourselves to
illuminate everything that is not honest, loving or healthy
for us. Over time we're able to identify the self-destructive
thoughts and habits that keep us running from or not
caring for ourselves. By making the choice to focus our
consciousness on how we feel now, we're empowered to
bring a loving presence deep into our being, which is the
only way to transform whatever is currently sabotaging our
health, happiness or capacity to connect authentically now.
Through relating to ourselves with this degree of kindness
and honesty, we eventually realize that the inner freedom
we're seeking is already available right here in this very
moment. It is simply accessible to the degree that we speak
and act based on our true feelings, needs and desires today.
Beyond liberating ourselves from the vicious cycles of feeling
held back by the past or being worried about the future,
through coming home to our breathing and body in this very
moment, we discover that there's always been an ocean of
love, peace, joy and wisdom within us beneath the anxiety,
insecurity, fear, confusion and unhappiness that torture us.

From a broader perspective, this moment is also our
pathway home to God, to the unlimited creative force of
the universe, which lives and has its being through us. In
other words, this moment is also where we experience our
oneness with the infinite, loving intelligence that created
and sustains all life on our planet as well as all that exists

throughout the entire universe. Practically speaking, when we're present to each breath, our inner wellspring of wisdom can expand from deep within us and provide us with the necessary insight to move forward in our personal growth and spiritual evolution. When we open our being to this ever-present source of clarity and knowing, we simultaneously open ourselves to the entire universal field of consciousness and energy that permeates everything that exists. This field that we're at one with, but most often closed to, then comes pouring through our being, supporting us and illuminating exactly what we must transform, heal and let go of in order to feel great within ourselves and enjoy our daily life. At the end of every spiritual discipline, once every thought has run its course back into the formless and unlimited potential from which it was born, we find that this moment exists eternally as the one and only gateway home to finding peace, health and loving connection. The suffering, restlessness, unhappiness and dis-ease that we experience are merely forms of homesickness guiding us to slow down, relax and simply enjoy the miracle of our life today.

If you will but turn to Me, and will carefully watch for and study these impressions which you are receiving every moment, and will learn to trust them, and thus to wait upon and rest in Me, putting all your faith in Me, verily I will guide you in all your ways; I will solve for you all your problems, make easy all your work, and you will be led among green pastures, beside the still waters of life.

The Impersonal Life

Practical Questions

In this moment, what are you feeling in your body, your heart and your mind? Do you feel tense, closed and anxious or relaxed, open and at peace?

How is the quality of your breathing? Is it deep and slow, or shallow and fast?

Can you breathe deeply and slowly into your lower belly and lower back?

Please try to and then notice what and how you feel.

Where in your body do you feel pain, tension or discomfort?

Can you focus your awareness on that area and then breathe deeply into it, allowing it to open and relax?

Do you believe that you are merely your thoughts and the voice in your head?

If so, then who and what is it inside of you that can observe the thoughts and voices in your head? Through focusing on your breath, can you feel the space, peace and stillness underneath your thoughts?

What does the word home mean to you?

Do you feel at home within yourself and also in your physical home?

Did you feel at home in your physical house growing up as a child? If not, why not?

Do you feel at home with the people you live with today?

What about the people you work with? If not, why not?

If you're not completely satisfied with your physical home, what does your ideal living environment look like and feel like?

Please describe it in as much detail as possible and please do not limit yourself in any way.

If you're not completely satisfied with your work environment, what does your ideal workspace look and feel like? Once again, please describe it in as much detail as possible and please do not limit yourself in any way.

(I highly recommend you write out your answers to these questions, because doing so will help you to create ideal living and working environments as soon as possible.)

Key Affirmations

I can feel good wherever I am.

My one true home is within my own body, heart and soul.

I am home. Welcome home [your name].

I am worthy and deserving of a beautiful, loving home.

I am so much more than the voice in my head.

Underneath my thoughts I am free, peaceful and full of love.

My physical pain and health concerns are guiding me home to my true self.

My breath is my pathway home in every moment.

CHAPTER 15

Inhale Life Deeply and Slowly

The mind can go in a thousand directions, but on this beautiful path, I walk in peace. With each step, the wind blows. With each step, a flower blooms ... Smile, breathe and go slowly.

Thich Nhat Hanh

Wherever you are, please take a few slow, deep breaths into your belly. Feel your whole body, from your feet all the way up to the crown of your head, and then down to your fingertips. Please relax any tension you feel and let yourself be. Using each inhalation to open your body and create inner space, welcome everything you're thinking, feeling and experiencing here in this moment. Please be present to your body and your breath.

If we can learn to be present to our breath in any given moment, we can find our way back to the strength, peace and love that already exist within us. Although we tend to overlook it, each inhalation offers a pathway down into the depths of our being, where unlimited space and stillness are always patiently waiting. Our breath is an anchor that has the power to keep us centred during the most turbulent of times. Regardless of how strong a thought or emotion is in our moment-to-moment experience, we'll always find a wealth of joy and clarity below these mental and emotional waves. Through our breath we can immediately step out of illusory thoughts about the past and future into the truth of life in the here and now. If we can intentionally practise dropping our awareness out of our head, by following our breath deep into our body, we can find acceptance, harmony and courage in any moment or situation.

The primary reason why most of us typically breathe at very shallow depths, specifically into our throat and upper chest, is because we've repressed and stored so many uncomfortable emotions deep within our body that we now fear feeling. However, by consciously focusing our attention on breathing slowly, deeply and fully, specifically into our belly, back and lungs, we can allow the energy that's become trapped in our head as confusion and obsessive thinking, as well as the energy that's trapped in our heart as anxiety and stress, to literally melt, drop and fill our body in a balanced and harmonious way. Truly to find the space, peace and stillness that exist deep within us, we must eventually make the challenging but necessary journey from our head down through our heart, into the very deepest parts of our being. At some point in our quest for lasting happiness and fulfilment, we must find the courage to feel all of the hurt, anxiety, anger, insecurity, fear, guilt and shame that we've shoved so deeply into the cells, organs and spaces that make up our physical body. The more deeply we breathe, the more deeply we feel, and it's only through feeling life deeply and fully that we can truly heal our body, heart and mind completely. In fact, there is a direct correlation between the fullness of our breath and the fullness of our lives, because we can only live our lives as fully as we're prepared to inhale the life force itself. In simple terms, the more fully we inhale the life-giving energy of oxygenated breath, the more we actually enjoy being alive each day.

> If you correct your mind, the rest of your life will fall into place.
>
> Lao Tzu

When we breathe in a shallow or anxious way, we not only allow our old emotional wounds to fester and become toxic, but we also allow ourselves to create additional pain on top of the unresolved emotions within us. When we look at the process of breathing in this light, it becomes clear that each moment actually offers us an opportunity to heal and be free by making a conscious choice to focus on inhaling life slowly, deeply and as fully as we can. We all know that human life would not be possible without oxygen, so if there's one thing that holds the power to give us more life and vitality than any other factor in our experience, our breath is by far the one. This is why intentionally breathing into every space inside our belly, back, chest and shoulders (*gently, without forcing it*) empowers us to fill these areas with the life-giving and life-healing energies that are infinitely available, everywhere, all of the time.

Through focusing our attention on inhaling deeply and slowly, we simultaneously allow our awareness to expand beyond our head so that it may fill every cell and corner of our being. The natural by-product of this process is a deep, tangible understanding of our unity with the ocean of energy and oxygen that fills all of the spaces and environments around us. Simply through breathing in life as gently and fully as possible, we begin to remember that we're not separate from anyone or anything that exists. Through mindful, deep breathing we eventually reawaken to our oneness with the universe and all life, and we also rediscover the infinite potential energy and life-giving force that exists in every particle, atom and molecule that surrounds us and gives form to our being.

All of us tend to make life much more difficult than it needs to be, mainly because we reject so much of what we think and feel. Then, we reactively say things and do things from a defensive place, which tends to create more hurt and separation. I think we all know that life is hard enough at times without us creating more pain or stress. I've come to realize that the emotional pain that we do everything in our power to avoid just continues to build up over time, making life *feel* much harder than it could be once we learn

Once you realize that the road is the goal, and that you are always on the road, not to reach a goal but to enjoy its beauty and its wisdom, life ceases to be a task and becomes natural and simple. In itself an ecstasy.

Nisargadatta Maharaj

to welcome, make space for and express all of what we feel.

For those of us who grew up feeling unloved, misunderstood or unsupported, life is indeed challenging while we're learning to love, honour, value and support ourselves. Thankfully, however, life actually becomes significantly easier when we stop resisting the flow of energy and emotion as it pulses throughout our being here in the present moment. In fact, once we learn to surrender fully to whatever we're thinking, feeling or experiencing, we naturally release our inner fight and accept whatever is occurring both within us and around us without struggling much at all.

It could be said that the single most important key to health and happiness is to master inhaling life deeply and slowly, because through intentionally cultivating this practice daily we can accept life as it is and allow life to unfold organically and enjoyably through every thought, emotion and experience. Personally, I have found that underneath all of my thoughts and emotions there is an ever-present source of peace and vital energy, and through consciously choosing to follow my breath deep into my body, I can find my way back to the inner freedom I desire in any moment or situation. As we welcome our experiences fully through our breath in each moment, we become one with our experience and thus quite effortlessly put an end to a significant amount of our suffering. By opening to life with each breath rather than contracting, we organically accept our unity with all that exists. As a direct result, the pain we've felt from feeling isolated, insecure, mistreated or unloved eventually melts away into the loving silence from which it came, and all we're left with are the joy and bliss of simply being alive.

Simple Deep-Breathing Meditation Practice

One of the most effective ways to cultivate ease and total acceptance of life in each moment and situation is through the following practice:

1. Gently place your tongue on the roof of your mouth. This connects two major energy channels/meridians in the body (used in traditional Chinese/Oriental medicine), which, once linked, create a harmonious, balanced and continuous flow of energy throughout the body.

2. Then, with your eyes either open or closed, depending on where you are and what you're doing, please inhale slowly, deeply and fully through your nose with the intention of filling your belly and lower back first, and then your chest, your upper back and your shoulders. You may even continue on and fill your throat and your head before exhaling slowing and gently out through your nose as well.

3. If for some reason your nose is clogged, you may inhale and exhale through your mouth. However, breathing through your nose for this practice is infinitely more effective in leading you to the peace, stillness and space deep inside your body.

4. When you notice your mind wandering while you are doing this practice, please simply say 'thinking' to yourself, and then bring your attention and your awareness back to your body and your breath. When you find yourself thinking about anyone or anything, or talking to yourself in any way, very gently just bring your focus back to inhaling slowly, deeply and fully.

5. Please do not judge, fight or resist any of your thoughts or emotions. Simply and kindly say 'thinking' when you notice you are not aware of your body or your breath and then shift your attention back to inhaling slowly, deeply and fully.

6. In any moment, you can consciously choose to come back to your body and your breath, and in so doing, you will always find deep peace, space and stillness underneath all of your thoughts and emotions.

7. Give yourself permission to let go and relax. Allow your body to open and release any stress or tension you're holding. Allow your breath to melt and heal any blocks or pain that you feel in your body.

8. Repeat this practice as often as you can throughout the day. It can be done sitting, standing or lying down for as long as you'd like. This practice is also great in the morning to wake you up as well as in the evening to relax your body, heart and mind.

9. **Additional step:** If you would like to take this meditation practice deeper, the following points will offer you structure and guidance to do so. Before you begin, I highly recommend finding a quiet place to sit where you will not be disturbed.

- **Creating time and space for a consistent meditation practice:** Each time you practise your meditation, please decide on a specific amount of time you feel comfortable committing to your practice. I recommend beginning with 10 minutes at first and then increasing your practice by 10-minute intervals each week until you can sit in meditation comfortably for 30–60 minutes. Please also find an alarm on your clock, watch or phone that you can use and set so that you're not constantly checking the time. Once you set the alarm and begin your practice, try not to check the time until the alarm goes off. Constantly checking the clock is just another subtle way of distracting ourselves from the present moment. Also, please put your phone(s) on silent so you won't be disturbed. Lastly, I highly recommend creating a consistent meditation practice in the morning before you leave your house, because it is the best way to create your day from a place of peace, positivity and clarity. Also, your thinking habits in the morning are the energy with which you create your day. So if your mental energy is all over the place, you will feel stressed, fragmented and spread thin. Conversely, through a simple short morning meditation, you can harness your thoughts and mental energy and then focus effectively on what you want to, need to and what feels good for you.

- **Effective meditation posture:** Whether you practise on a chair, bench, couch, meditation cushion or floor, please make sure you are sitting up straight and that your posture feels centred and balanced. You can sit back in your chair if this feels most natural; however, please make sure you're gently extending up throughout your spine so your vertebrae are not under too much pressure. At the same time, please relax all the muscles in your lower, middle and upper back so there's no additional tension being created in your body. It's also helpful to imagine a string attached to the crown of your head that's gently pulling you up and taking the pressure off your spine. In regards to your head position, it's best to look straight ahead and then very slightly tilt your chin down.

In regards to your legs and feet, if you are sitting on a chair, couch or bench, it's best to have both feet flat on the floor, as this helps ground and balance the energy in your body. It's also helpful to have your knees at a 90-degree angle so the energy and blood in your legs can flow freely. If your knees are too high above your pelvis, the energy and blood will get stuck around your hips and you'll feel uncomfortable while practising your meditation. Thus, if you have long legs or are sitting on a small chair, this can be remedied by putting a pillow under you to boost you up a bit. If, on the other hand, your feet do not touch the floor for any reason, it's helpful to put a pillow under your feet. If you're sitting on the floor, or on a meditation cushion, it is best to have your legs crossed. Once again, it's ideal to have your knees lower than your pelvis so the energy and blood can flow freely without getting stuck. Thus, if your hip-flexors and groin muscles are tight, it's best to sit on a pillow or meditation cushion to ensure that your pelvis is higher than your knees.

In regards to the position of your hands, it is best to have them either palms down on your thighs or together in your lap in some way. If you have them together in your lap, I recommend gently interlacing your fingers. Ultimately, it's important to find a position that feels good for you so you can remain still throughout your meditation practice.

- **Eyes open versus eyes closed:** The last key point to address in deepening your meditation practice relates to your eyes being either open or closed while you practise. Both approaches are very effective, and they both deserve equal attention. Practising with our eyes open is very important because it helps us cultivate our ability to 'be in the world' consciously without being reactive. Ultimately, we want to bring the peace found through meditation into our daily lives, so meditating with our eyes open helps us bring more presence, awareness and love into every moment, experience and relationship. Practising with our eyes closed is also important because it encourages us to go deeper into the peace, stillness, love and awareness within us. It is very nourishing to close off completely to the outside world and then dive deeply into our being.

When meditating with your eyes open, the best approach is to look down towards the ground about 4–6 ft (1.5–1.8m) in front of you. It's best not to look at any one point in particular but rather to relax both your eyes and your gaze on the general area in front of you. When we fixate ('zoom in') on a particular point on the floor it's the same as fixating on a thought in our mind, so any time you find yourself fixating on a spot or piece of dirt on the floor, please treat this experience as a thought, say 'thinking' to yourself, relax your gaze ('zoom out'), and then return your awareness to your breathing and your body. When meditating with our eyes open, it's best to direct 95 per cent of our awareness inwards and only 5 per cent outwards. The idea is to be visually aware of the 180-degree perspective in front of you while remaining fully aware of your body, breath and thinking processes as well. In the beginning, this technique can feel a bit awkward, but in time it becomes more natural and leads to extremely deep levels of peace and self-awareness.

When meditating with your eyes closed, simply close your eyes and follow the next step outlined below.

- **Closing points:** After finding the meditation posture
  that works best for you and setting your alarm, please
  follow steps one through seven from the simple deep-
  breathing meditation practice on pages 167–168. After
  inhaling and exhaling slowly, deeply and fully for a few
  minutes, please allow your breathing to become natural
  and uncontrolled. Then, rest your awareness on your
  breath so you can observe each inhalation and each
  exhalation while simultaneously feeling your whole
  body. In deepening your meditation, please focus on
  steps four through seven from the practice on pages
  162–3, but allow your breathing to be completely natural
  and unforced. As described earlier, when you find your
  mind wandering and notice yourself thinking about
  anything or anyone, please say 'thinking' to yourself and
  then gently bring your attention and focus back to each
  inhalation and exhalation, and to feeling your whole
  body as you breathe.

In the end, there is no right or wrong way to practise
your meditation. What matters is your commitment to
(1) remaining present to all your thoughts, emotions and
physical sensations, (2) feeling each breath come in and
go out, and (3) welcoming everything that arises with
loving-kindness, acceptance and compassion.

While deepening your meditation practice, it's very
helpful to know that physical irritation and discomfort
often arise as blocks or sabotages to self-mastery and
self-love. Most of us have a large amount of repressed
psychological and emotional irritation and discomfort
stored within us, which initially surfaces during
meditation as physical agitation and restlessness
before it can be healed. Thus, it is crucial to surrender

and accept the physical discomfort that arises as you lengthen your practice, because this is the only way to heal the underlying emotional discomfort that needs to be liberated before you can find lasting inner peace and happiness. With this in mind, it is important to stay committed, persistent and patient with your meditation practice, even if agitation, irritation or discomfort arise.

Lastly, I highly recommend re-reading this particular chapter after you've practised the meditation a few times. It will continually offer guidance and clarity as you master loving yourself unconditionally and come home fully to life in the present moment.

You are told to love your neighbour as yourself. How do you love yourself? When I look into my own mind, I find that I do not love myself by thinking myself a dear old chap or having affectionate feelings. I do not think that I love myself because I am particularly good, but just because I am myself and quite apart from my character. I might detest something which I have done. Nevertheless, I do not cease to love myself. In other words, that definite distinction that Christians make between hating sin and loving the sinner is one that you have been making in your own case since you were born. You dislike what you have done, but you don't cease to love yourself. You may even think that you ought to be hanged. You may even think that you ought to go to the police and own up and be hanged. Love is not [just] affectionate feeling, but a steady wish for the loved person's ultimate good as far as it can be obtained.

C S Lewis

CHAPTER 16

Unconditional Self-Love

What can we gain by sailing to the moon if we are not able to cross the abyss that separates us from ourselves?

Thomas Merton

Wherever you are, please take a few slow, deep breaths into your belly. Feel your whole body, from your feet all the way up to the crown of your head, and then down to your fingertips. Please relax any tension you feel and let yourself be. Using each inhalation to open your body and create inner space, welcome everything you're thinking, feeling and experiencing here in this moment. Please be present to your body and your breath.

When we look closely at our relationship with ourselves, we see that most of us live in a way in which we only love ourselves 'if' and 'when' we meet certain conditions that we've created for ourselves and then projected on to some distant future or some long-gone past.

- I will love myself 'if' I'm in a loving relationship.
- I will love myself 'when' I become successful.
- I will love myself 'if' I lose weight.
- I will love myself 'when' I make more money.
- I will love myself 'if' I get that degree.
- I will love myself 'when' I have that new car or that new house.
- I would love myself 'if' I didn't have wrinkles.
- I would love myself 'if' I didn't have this illness or this disability.

Does this conversation sound familiar?

Because most of us never learned how to love and value ourselves in the present, just the way we are, we constantly look to a fantasy reality in the future where we think we'll be more lovable, more deserving of love, or more able to love ourselves than we do right now. Less often, some of us even take this dynamic and turn it around by looking back on our past with regretful thoughts ('I used to love myself when ...' or 'I would love myself if I looked like I did back when ...'). In these rarer cases our conditions keep us stuck in guilt, regret or resentment over what has been and gone and therefore no longer is. Regardless of where we place our conditions, if we continue to relate to ourselves in conditional ways, we'll never get to the future place or the past place where we're finally ready to love ourselves here in the present. We have to begin to love ourselves now in order to create, accomplish or find what we desire most in life. It is never the other way around, despite how much we believe it to be so.

Looking to the future in order to love ourselves more in the present will never help us transform what we have not been able to love already within ourselves, our lives or our past. Similarly, holding on to situations, relationships or images of the past that are loaded with regret or denial will never help us to create healthy, happy lives here in the present either. What we do not love, accept or honour in this moment will always remain beneath the surface of our awareness until we honestly face it, forgive it, understand it and therefore heal it. Regardless of how far we try to run from ourselves or how strongly we deny this dynamic, it will constantly stop us from finding peace, health, happiness and true love, while simultaneously driving us to create situations that are full of additional pain and confusion.

Our conditional love for ourselves is generally rooted in deep feelings and limiting beliefs around not being 'enough' or 'worthy of love' just as we are, which leaves many of us feeling we must always be more, do more or have more to finally be lovable to ourselves and to others. At the core of this self-destructive internal dynamic is the fact that when we were growing up most of our parents could not love us unconditionally, just as we were, because they did not love themselves unconditionally just as they were. So not only did we inherit love-deprived beliefs, emotions and habits at birth, but many of us were also raised in homes where no matter how much we tried to please our parents or make them happy, nothing would ever or could ever be 'enough' to satisfy their own insecurities, inadequacies, dissatisfaction and unreasonable expectations.

Now, depending on how unhappy and disappointed our parents were in themselves, we've all lived believing that we're not good enough, smart enough, successful enough, attractive enough, loving enough or selfless enough. And this is why we find ourselves in situations today that feel the same way we felt as children growing up. Often we try to make others happy or please their every wish, because we hold this deeply rooted belief that this is the only way to live. But the truth is, we've lived unaware that another way of life exists outside of the self-imposed limitations and conditions we inherited during childhood.

Understanding this dynamic is in no way encouragement to blame our parents or to feel sorry for ourselves. It's simply a logical view on the root causes of many of our struggles; struggles which our parents endured their whole life as well, because like all of us, their parents didn't know better either. For generations, the majority of the population has remained unaware of how to live in a way where they feel connected to their inherent wholeness and worth. We rarely hear, even as adults, that we are not only worthy of love –

no matter what – but also, that who we truly are beyond our limiting beliefs already is pure love. That's why we all want and need love so deeply, and this is also why love, in a healthy form, always feels so good and so liberating. *We're all simply looking for the love that we are so that we can just be the love that we are. We're all intuitively looking for ourselves so we can just be ourselves.*

Unaware of this, however, we're still placing ourselves under constant pressure and creating our lives from a mindset of lack, unworthiness and inadequacy. We constantly hurt ourselves for the love of other people, always trying to please them and keep them happy because we mistakenly believe this is still the only way to survive or get by. Meanwhile, our true needs, desires and dreams continually get ignored because we don't think we're worthy of having what we genuinely value or envisage for ourselves. Fortunately, however, each of us is actually destined to wake up from this perceptual nightmare and then heal ourselves by letting go of the limiting conditions that we continuously place on our own love for ourselves. A key to achieving this is understanding that beneath all the limiting conditions we create or take on there is simply repressed emotional pain, which is the result of all the times in the past that we have not related to ourselves with the honesty, acceptance and kindness we need.

Our limiting beliefs around being inadequate, unworthy or undeserving in any way paradoxically exist to protect us from the uncomfortable emotions that we ourselves have created and stored within our being. They also exist to create contrast and thus give us an idea of what the opposite and adequate feeling is. All the aspects of our life that are or were painful – that we judge, reject, deny, hide, run from, fear, feel insecure about, ashamed of, angry about, regretful for or guilty about – are the obstacles that block us from feeling and knowing our true nature, which is always enough, always whole and never lacking in anything. Once we learn to be kind and true to ourselves with each word and action, we stop creating knots and blockages in a body that is designed for an infinite amount of life and love.

From a broader perspective, when our love for ourselves is conditional in nature, so too are the peace and happiness that we experience on a daily basis. Underneath the conditions that we all place on ourselves as to 'if' and 'when' we'll finally be at peace or happy are really the conditions that we place on ourselves as to 'if' and 'when' we'll finally be lovable to ourselves and to others. When we live believing that we'll only be lovable 'if' and 'when' we meet certain conditions that are not present now, we're in effect giving our peace and happiness away to these unhealthy thoughts, which always translates into not enjoying life now. In the same way that we search for love outside of ourselves when we don't know how to love ourselves now or address our deeper wounds, we also look for peace and happiness outside of ourselves when we're not at peace, happy or satisfied with *who we are, who we've been, or with the life we've created.* So whether we're looking for love, or for peace and happiness, we're always led back to mastering life's most important lesson, which entails learning to accept, value and be true to ourselves today, regardless of where we are, what we've done or where we want to go.

It doesn't matter how many goals we achieve, how much money we make, how great our body looks or how many good deeds we do; we will always find ourselves faced with the same parts of ourselves, our lives and our past that we still do not feel good about or at peace with. Through our struggles with our health, addictive behaviour, close relationships or finances, our soul is calling out for us to drop our limiting conditions so that we can finally heal our heart and thus stop living in our head focused on an illusion of the future.

When we finally stop running from past hurt, it's easy to see how we create self-destructive conditions in the present to protect us and distract us from what remains unresolved within us. However, as we slow down enough to drop out of our head into the depth and wholeness of our being, to our surprise we find an ocean of loving wisdom and strength beneath all the negative beliefs and feelings that we hold within and towards ourselves. In this revelation comes a desire for deeper surrender into this truth, where we finally stop cutting ourselves off from feeling secure and enough. Once we're clear on how our habits of holding everything in lead us to feel insecure, inadequate and trapped in the vicious cycle of conditional love, we naturally don't want to hurt ourselves further. This is where we really come to see every limiting condition that we place on our peace, happiness and love for ourselves as just a fear-based pattern of thought that we're using as an excuse not to be true to ourselves now, which obviously does not serve us any more.

Practical Questions

What conditions do you place on yourself as to 'if' and 'when' you will finally love yourself here in the present moment?

What conditions do you place on yourself as to 'if' and 'when' you will finally be at peace, happy and fulfilled?

What stories do you tell yourself about why you are not lovable?

What negative beliefs do you hold about yourself that block you from loving yourself now?

What about you, your life, or your past justifies you feeling unworthy or undeserving of love?

Do you always feel you must be more, do more and have more, finally to feel lovable to yourself and to others?

Do you always feel you must be more, do more, and have more, finally to be at peace, happy or satisfied within yourself and your life?

Do you think your mother and father loved themselves unconditionally? If not, can you see that it was hard for them to love you unconditionally and to teach you how to love yourself unconditionally?

Do you feel you always had to be more, do more or have more so that your parents would love you or so they would be happy and satisfied? Can you see how your conditional love for yourself began at a very early age?

Where, right now, is fear stopping you from speaking and acting based on your true feelings, needs and desires?

Can you finally love and value yourself now by being true to yourself, even if you're scared?

Key Affirmations

I am lovable just as I am.

To feel good enough and worthy of love, I need to be honest and true to myself in each situation.

I do not need to be more, do more or have more to feel good about myself.

I deserve love in my life. I always have and I always will.

I forgive my parents for not teaching me to love myself unconditionally.

I forgive my parents for not being able to love, accept and support me unconditionally.

I now choose to relate to myself with unconditional love, kindness and compassion in every moment, situation and relationship.

The past and future are not real. All I ever have is now, and all the love I need is already alive within me.

I love myself now by speaking and acting honestly.

I will not wait to value myself or to be happy.

To feel love and respect for myself in the future, I need to be true to myself today.

CHAPTER 17

Overcome Self-Judgement and Rejection

And those who were seen dancing were thought to be insane by those who could not hear the music.

Friedrich Nietzsche

Wherever you are, please take a few slow, deep breaths into your belly. Feel your whole body, from your feet all the way up to the crown of your head, and then down to your fingertips. Please relax any tension you feel and let yourself be. Using each inhalation to open your body and create inner space, welcome everything you're thinking, feeling and experiencing here in this moment. Please be present to your body and your breath.

We all judge ourselves, and at times we all judge others. In both cases, our judgements exist merely to protect us from feeling the uncomfortable emotions that we've repressed throughout our lives. Through judging other people we temporarily make ourselves feel better about what we judge and don't feel good about in ourselves. We only judge others to distract us from what we struggle to accept about ourselves and our own lives. Like all people, beyond our own self-judgements, our true self is still deserving of respect, regardless of what we believe makes us unlovable. When we judge ourselves to be inadequate or undeserving in any way, the reality is we've merely lost touch with the space and awareness within us that not only embraces our darkness and our light, but also understands its purpose and values its presence.

We all briefly forget the limitlessness of our true nature, but eventually we're destined to know this deep inner truth once again. To free ourselves from suffering and enjoy our lives, our lesson is to acknowledge and accept the many different aspects of who, where and how we've been. Even if we feel deep shame around something, each of us is challenged to own our most vulnerable emotions, thoughts, desires and experiences.

If we look honestly at the ways we relate to ourselves today, the majority of us will discover that there are many things that we judge, reject, hide and run from. Most of us do not welcome all of what we think, feel, want and need. As we've seen before, these patterns around judging, rejecting and denying our inner truths began building when we were very young because we feared losing the love and support we needed in our early years. Prior to our awakening and healing, many of us have lived our entire lives totally unaware of how far we've moved away from who we really are because we never learned how to accept and honour all of our feelings all the time.

In trying to understand the root causes of self-rejection and self-judgement, one could say that even upon our conception and throughout our mother's pregnancy, we learned about the nature of love through the lens of unhealthy, limiting conditions. Most of us were conceived in the energy of what our parents believed and felt to be love, both for themselves and for others, at that particular point in their personal growth and evolution. More specifically, when it comes to the relationship that our parents had with themselves and the degree to which they truly accepted themselves at the time of our conception, it was often not the healthiest dynamic, because this is true for most people. We could go so far as to say that the nature of the relationship we each have towards ourselves today has its roots stretching back biologically through our genetic line and spiritually through lifetimes' worth of karma.

Whether you believe in reincarnation or not, the truth is that this lifetime contains everything we need to address and learn to be completely free and happy. In fact, because both the unresolved past and the seeds of our future are present now it's more practical to understand that the people who birthed us and raised us could not give us what they themselves were never given or had not learned for themselves. Our parents and most of the people who influenced us growing up did not accept themselves entirely, so logically it follows that they could not completely accept us or show us how to relate to ourselves in this kind and compassionate way – even if they truly wanted to. Although this dynamic has been many people's experience, we still cannot afford to waste our time or energy blaming our parents, or anyone else, for the lack of love we have for ourselves in the present. Our parents, along with every other person alive, struggled to accept themselves unconditionally, whether they were conscious of this inner reality or not. As human beings, we're all challenged by the inner relationship we have with ourselves, regardless of whether or not we express this vulnerable inner truth. This is why we're all called to find a place of compassionate understanding within ourselves where we release all blame and accept all of who we are now.

> Out beyond our ideas of wrong-doing and right-doing,
> There is a field. I will meet you there.
> When the soul lies down in that grass,
> The world is too full to talk about.
> Ideas, language, even the phrase 'each other' doesn't make
>   any sense.

Jalaluddin Rumi

We've all developed unconscious fears around being judged and rejected by other people because we fear feeling the emotional pain we associate with these experiences. What we typically don't understand is that the pain from rejecting ourselves is far more damaging and hurtful than being rejected by another person could ever be. In fact, most of the sadness that surfaces when we feel rejected or judged by another person is actually the accumulated result of all the times in the past that we did not accept or honour ourselves. Anyone who judges or rejects us only does so because they are still judging and rejecting themselves, so their reaction to us actually has little to do with us. As we learn to be true to ourselves each day, which in large part is self-acceptance in action, whether people accept or judge us has less and less effect on how we feel about ourselves.

Until we realize how exhausting living in fear truly is, we judge, reject and hurt ourselves in the exact ways we subconsciously fear being hurt by other people. We're obviously not aware of it, but this self-destructive dynamic has created countless inner battles between who we really are and the person we've become to be accepted, approved of and supported throughout our lives. Far more than losing love from other people, our deeper fear surrounds feeling all the repressed emotional pain that has built up within us over so many years of trying to be someone or something that we're not, just to please other people.

The longer we allow ourselves to deny what we feel, need and desire, the longer we remain disconnected from our authentic self and the more frustrating, depressed and toxic our lives become. If we really want to find peace and self-respect, and to enjoy our lives, we're called to forgive ourselves for not accepting ourselves in the past and to commit to not rejecting ourselves again. As young children, we didn't know how to accept ourselves or stick up for ourselves. But you and I are not small kids any more, and we have both the power and the awareness to face and feel everything we've disconnected from. We all have the strength and courage within to finally embody the wholeness of who we are.

Moving forward in our evolution as a human being is the process by which what is unconscious or fragmented within us becomes both conscious and integrated. This expansion in our awareness and felt sense of inner space is necessary to move beyond mere survival to thrive in harmony with all aspects of our life. This is true adaptation with respect to effectively navigating our internal and external environments, and it is also the key to maintaining strong instinct and intuition. Another way of saying this is that our personal growth, health and happiness depend upon our willingness to welcome all that we've judged, rejected and hidden in the past. For this reason, each moment offers us an opportunity to accept what we feel, think, want and need without allowing our fears to result in more self-rejection and thus more suffering. The majority of our self-criticism actually results from denying our true self, because in doing so we are lying to ourselves and to others. Then, we give ourselves a hard time for doing so. This is why finding the courage to speak and act based on our true feelings now is the most practical expression of accepting all of who we are as well as the most direct path to enjoying our life.

Practical Questions

What do you judge, reject, deny or hide about yourself
in the present?

What do you judge, reject, deny or hide about your life
in the present?

What do you judge, reject, deny or hide about yourself
from the past?

What do you judge, reject, deny or hide about your life
from the past?

When you observe yourself with other people, what do you
typically judge about them? Can you see how this mirrors what
you judge about yourself?

What are your core insecurities right now?

What do you fear people knowing about you, your life or your
past? Do you have any secrets that you hide from everyone or
from certain people? If so, who do you hide them from and why?

If you could travel back in time and speak to yourself as a child,
what would you say to him or her in regards to being true to
yourself all of the time?

What can you focus your energy on today that represents you
accepting what you love to do, want to do or need to do?

Key Affirmations

It's okay that I judge myself sometimes.

When I judge myself or other people, I'm just protecting myself from pain.

I accept my whole self. I welcome my darkness and my light.

I do not need to deny my wholeness to be loved.

I am lovable just the way I am. I deserve to be loved for who I really am.

I can live my life for me. I'm not here to please others or to make them happy.

I am here to be myself and to enjoy my life.

Accepting myself means accepting and honouring my feelings, thoughts, needs and dreams.

CHAPTER 18

Forgive Yourself Now

You who want peace can find it only by complete forgiveness.

A Course in Miracles

Wherever you are, please take a few slow, deep breaths into your belly. Feel your whole body, from your feet all the way up to the crown of your head, and then down to your fingertips. Please relax any tension you feel and let yourself be. Using each inhalation to open your body and create inner space, welcome everything you're thinking, feeling and experiencing here in this moment. Please be present to your body and your breath.

Deep down we're all good, loving people, and yet we all live with things that we've said or done that we struggle to forgive. Regardless of how bad, guilty, ashamed, angry or regretful we feel about past situations or decisions, we must eventually understand that each experience was ultimately awakening us to our true self and to the purpose of our lives. If we've unconsciously acted in ways that have caused ourselves or others pain, it's always because we had lessons to learn so we could evolve and grow in a loving presence and awareness. The shame, guilt, anger and regret that we still feel and store subconsciously in our body hold jewels of wisdom that are waiting to teach us about what's most important in life – about truth, honesty, forgiveness, acceptance and unconditional love.

If we do not open to forgiving the things in our past that we still feel shame, guilt, anger or regret around, then these aspects of our lives will stop us from finding lasting inner peace and happiness. The toxic emotions that are tied up with what remains unforgiven will drive us to create additional experiences in which we feel negatively about ourselves and our lives. We'll continually create painful situations in the present until we realize that we're destined to forgive ourselves and move forward with our lives.

Regardless of how bad we feel about past actions, we're all capable and deserving of forgiveness. Each of us deserves to be forgiven for the pain we've caused other people, but we won't be able to openly accept or receive this forgiveness until we understand why we acted in the ways we did. Even in situations where the person who feels hurt by our actions has not forgiven us, we can still forgive ourselves, face the guilt or shame, and grow from the experience. Everything that we do or experience in this life is meant for us to learn from, including what we perceive to be our mistakes. In fact, our so-called mistakes are actually the most important life lessons that we've needed to learn in order to grow in awareness, humility and compassion. If we truly want to heal and be happy, we need to understand the lessons inherent within the painful situations we've created, because this awareness is what eventually allows us to untie the knots of shame, guilt, anger and regret that are connected to these past experiences.

It can indeed be difficult to forgive ourselves when we've unintentionally hurt people we love or have loved deeply. Equally, it can be challenging to forgive ourselves when we're being blamed for more than we're actually responsible for in what's become a painful situation. But at some point, regardless of how much suffering we've caused, or are perceived to have caused, we have to come to forgive ourselves, because our repressed feelings about the situation will not only hold us back and keep us miserable; they will also lead to toxicity in every cell of our body and every situation in our lives. Through forgiving ourselves we actually open the space for loving-kindness to shine through our thoughts, actions and spoken words, which is much better for the world than us being trapped in shame, guilt or regret. This is how we grow in wisdom and organically stop acting or reacting in unconscious ways that result in pain for ourselves or others.

A person will be called to account on Judgement Day for every permissible thing he might have enjoyed but did not.

The Talmud

Beyond forgiving ourselves for the pain we've caused other people, we must learn to forgive ourselves for the pain that is at the source of all the pain we've ever created in our lives. We must go back through each stage of our lives and forgive ourselves for compromising, betraying and hurting ourselves for the conditional love, acceptance, approval and support of other people. We must go back in time and forgive ourselves for neglecting who we truly are, because this pain that we've been inflicting upon ourselves since we were children is actually the underlying reason for all the pain we've ever created or allowed.

To find lasting inner peace, health and happiness we must eventually forgive ourselves for rejecting our true self to please others. We're called to forgive ourselves for being so hard, so critical and so aggressive with ourselves. We have to forgive ourselves for making ourselves wrong and for running from our true feelings so regularly. This process only deepens, because we need to forgive ourselves for taking on external conditions as to 'if' and 'when' we'll finally love ourselves in our entirety. We have to forgive ourselves for all the pain, confusion and frustration we've created for ourselves by living from a place of fear. Finally, we're all challenged to accept, value, respect and be true to ourselves in every situation so we do not hurt ourselves any more, but rather create a healthy, happy and authentic life where there's no longer anything to forgive.

The one master key to understanding *how to forgive ourselves* is this: do not hurt yourself again or allow yourself to be hurt by others. When you speak and act with kindness and honesty in each situation, you stop betraying yourself and you stop allowing yourself to stay in unhealthy situations. Then the loving truth behind your words and actions can heal past hurt from the inside out without being sabotaged by new self-created pain.

Practical Questions

What in your life right now do you feel guilt, shame, anger
or regret about?

What do you still feel guilt, shame, anger or regret about
from your past?

Can you see how the only reason you've ever hurt another person
is because you were hurting or confused in yourself and thus
avoiding the truth in some way?

Where do you still compromise yourself and abandon your true
feelings, needs and desires?

Where have you betrayed yourself in the past?

Where do you still judge yourself in your life?

How are you still hard on yourself right now?

What can you focus your energy on today that represents
you valuing yourself and therefore honouring what you love
to do, want to do or need to do?

Key Affirmations

Deep down I know I am a good person.

Everything happens for a reason.

I forgive myself for the hurt I've caused others.

I forgive myself for hurting [name the person(s) you've hurt].

My mistakes in life have been purposeful and necessary.

I forgive myself for not knowing how to love myself.

I forgive myself for the pain and disrespect I have allowed.

I forgive myself for not being true to myself and for not valuing myself.

CHAPTER 19

Transform Anger, Hurt and Hatred

You will not be punished for your anger, you will be punished by your anger. Holding on to anger is like grasping a hot coal with the intent of throwing it at someone else; you are the one who gets burned.

Buddha

Wherever you are, please take a few slow, deep breaths into your belly. Feel your whole body, from your feet all the way up to the crown of your head, and then down to your fingertips. Please relax any tension you feel and let yourself be. Using each inhalation to open your body and create inner space, welcome everything you're thinking, feeling and experiencing here in this moment. Please be present to your body and your breath.

We have all hurt other people with our words and actions. This is why we grow in our capacity to forgive others as we learn to forgive ourselves. If, however, we have not honestly owned what we see to be our own mistakes and therefore learned the purposeful lessons inherent within these experiences, then we'll continuously struggle to forgive others for what we still perceive to be their imperfections, especially the ones we feel have hurt us personally. It's not until we truly forgive ourselves that we open up to understanding that everyone is still learning and growing. As we deepen our own awareness into how and why we ourselves have created situations in the past where we've caused pain, either to ourselves or to others, we simultaneously grow in compassion for other people.

Eventually, we realize that the only reason why we ourselves or anyone else would ever create pain for another person is because deep down we're hurting, confused and reacting. As we come to understand our own choices and our own actions more deeply, we also gain insight into why others have acted or continue to act in ways that have caused or still cause us pain. This new level of understanding other people makes it possible for us to forgive them, especially when we can see how scared or unaware they are or were.

If we're truly honest with ourselves, in time, we all come to realize that we're no different and no better than anyone else, so to judge anyone as 'wrong' or 'bad', for any reason, is simply another subtle form of unconscious destructive behaviour. Everyone, including you and me, is just looking for love, connection, security, understanding and happiness, even when we create serious chaos or pain in the process.

From a strictly self-interested perspective, forgiving others is actually much healthier than holding on to anger, resentment or hatred, because these negative and aggressive emotions only eat away at our own health, happiness and wellbeing. They also block us from moving forward in our own lives. This is why it's so important to face the hurt, anger, resentment and hatred we hold personally towards other people or groups, because whenever we allow ourselves to live with this pain for extended periods of time we're literally giving our life and our joy away through this subtle form of victimhood. By asserting justifications for why we cannot take complete responsibility for our own inner peace and happiness right now, we ultimately just make ourselves more sick and miserable, regardless of how the person we expect to feel bad or guilty actually feels. When we finally find the strength, wisdom and humility to forgive others and move on with our lives, however, we can easily reclaim our energy to enjoy life selfishly and focus on all that we love.

When another person makes you suffer, it is because he suffers deeply within himself, and his suffering is spilling over. He does not need punishment; he needs help.

Thich Nhat Hanh

Eventually, you'll see clearly that in order to love yourself wholeheartedly and enjoy your life, you must embody the unconditional love that you are by bringing true forgiveness into the world. When it comes to forgiving other people, we're always brought full circle back to forgiving ourselves. Whenever we've experienced hurt in relation to another person, it's almost always because we've allowed it to happen. It's nearly always because we were unaware to some degree, most likely compromising, abandoning or betraying ourselves in some way to please another.

If we still feel deeply hurt by someone for any reason, the heart of the issue always comes back to us not knowing how to value and be true to ourselves in some way. And the only way to move forward now is to speak and act from a place of honesty, kindness and self-respect, because doing so is how we heal the past and move forward. Knowing this, please forgive yourself for what you've let happen. You didn't know any better. You were learning, just as we all are. Please also open to forgiving those who you feel have hurt you in some way. They too are still learning. As we addressed previously, the key to forgiving both ourselves and others is to never reject or betray ourselves again. At this stage in life, you can stick up for yourself, take responsibility for your life, and never allow yourself to become a victim of another person's unconsciousness again. Through being completely true to yourself, even when you're afraid, all will be forgiven and you will finally be free to enjoy your life. If you must choose between being happy or remaining stuck in hurt, anger and hate, which will you choose?

Practical Questions

Are there people in your life who you feel have hurt, betrayed, violated or wronged you in some way? Who are these people that you feel anger, resentment or hatred towards and why do you feel the way you do?

Have you forgiven these people completely for the pain you feel they have caused you? If not, why not? Are you ready to forgive them, forgive yourself and move forward with your life?

Has anyone broken your heart whom you have not forgiven?

Do you hate anyone or anything? If so, who, what and why?

Do you truly want to give your health, happiness and peace away to the people who have hurt you or not valued you in the past?

Can you see how in each situation and relationship where you've felt hurt or taken advantage of, you've actually betrayed yourself in some way? Can you forgive yourself for not knowing how to speak and act from your true feelings?

Where do you need to speak and act based on your true feelings, needs and desires today so that you stop hurting yourself or allowing yourself to be hurt?

Key Affirmations

Please make a list of every person towards whom you feel anger, resentment, hurt or hatred. Then, please use their names with the following affirmation:

I forgive [person's name], and I set myself free.

I forgive myself for being unaware. I forgive myself for not loving myself.

I am love, and love naturally forgives.

I too have acted in ways that have hurt other people. How can I not try to forgive?

I can forgive without being naïve. I can forgive and also value myself moving forward.

I'm ready to forgive and move forward with my life's purpose.

I forgive myself for seeking other people's love, acceptance, approval and support, to my own detriment.

CHAPTER 20

Follow Your Heart

If everyone approves of what you are doing,
I urge you to reconsider what you are doing.

Saint Germain

Wherever you are, please take a few slow, deep breaths into your belly. Feel your whole body, from your feet all the way up to the crown of your head, and then down to your fingertips. Please relax any tension you feel and let yourself be. Using each inhalation to open your body and create inner space, welcome everything you're thinking, feeling and experiencing here in this moment. Please be present to your body and your breath.

Every desire in our heart is the evolutionary impulse of life and nature driving us forward towards lasting inner peace, happiness and the realization of our full potential. The desires in our heart are in fact the desires of God, the desires of the intelligent universe, to know itself and express itself through our lives. Contrary to our limiting beliefs, we are very capable of creating, having or achieving the desires that persist in our heart over time. We simply have to find the self-worth to value ourselves and thus not settle for anything less. Every strong desire that we experience contains a vital lesson we must learn in order to find the courage to be true to ourselves, bring unconditional love into the world and simply enjoy being alive each day.

Some schools of thought teach that desire leads to suffering and thus should be repressed or not acted upon. But in my experience this is not the whole truth. Desire leads to suffering when we're attached to getting what we want because we're trying to avoid ourselves, our suffering or a specific situation. Desire can also lead to suffering when we need to learn a critical lesson that will later serve us greatly. However, when we address our true feelings in the present and also face our unresolved emotional wounds from the past, we can simultaneously feel the desire to create, enjoy and achieve certain things without it leading to pain.

Desire that is free from denial and fear actually leads to joy, healthy creative expression and peace. The evolutionary force of the universe, which is alive inside every one of our cells, is always guiding us forward towards the health and happiness we seek *through our desires*. Regardless of how hard we try, the universe's desire to express itself through our physical existence cannot be stopped, because you and I are both one with, and also the result of, this creative force and intelligence that deeply desires to know itself and enjoy itself through everyone and everything that comes into being. We cannot stop desire from surfacing within us. Even if what we desire initially causes us pain, ironically, it is the desire itself that eventually forces us to face the underlying causes of our suffering. If, for a period, we desire large amounts of pleasure merely to avoid what's difficult in our lives, at some stage we'll realize that our focus is not bringing the lasting peace, happiness or relief we thought it would. As we face this fact fully we can accept the uncomfortable emotions we've been avoiding or numbing ourselves to, and then finally heal them. This process naturally gives rise to a purer form of desire, which then guides us to enjoy life and love with peace and truth in our heart.

If we continually deny what we desire, we just end up repressing the life and the love that are trying to express themselves through us. By rejecting our desires, we unintentionally reject the lessons and the healing towards which our desires are driving us. Often we're also simply rejecting the truth, which leads us to live a lie. For so many reasons, it is always in our best interest to address what we truly want so that we can learn the lessons we need to learn and embody what is wholeheartedly honest for us. Whether our initial desire is for food, alcohol, drugs, sex, money, attention, fame, recognition, love or freedom, honouring this inner truth, even if it causes us pain, is better than constantly denying the desire's existence, because it's only through excessive craving for anything or anyone that we eventually find balance and learn to value moderation and self-discipline. Like a bird that continually flies into a glass window and hurts itself because it does not see the window, we too must go after things that create pain before we naturally choose not to. This is how we learn to value our time and energy more, and feel at peace with our choice.

To enjoy our lives deeply, we also have to go after what we desire so we can see through the illusion that it will somehow make us happy or fulfil us forever. There's no way around this unless we trap ourselves in a cave, and even then most of us won't truly find what we're looking for. Through following our heart, we eventually realize exactly what we need to realize about what supports our overall wellbeing and love for ourselves, and what does not, because it's only through trial and error that we finally learn to enjoy life each day without doing so self-destructively. This dance between what we desire and the associated pleasure and pain always leads to a clear understanding of the universe's perfectly designed plan to wake us up and help us remember that all of the peace, happiness, freedom and love we desire will only be found within ourselves.

We cannot repress our desires in the hope of avoiding pain, because we can never free ourselves from suffering by avoiding our suffering. Genuine happiness is only found by courageously stepping into the heart of our pain with unconditional love for ourselves. Our challenge is always to follow our inner voice, because as we do so, the love within us naturally heals and fulfils our deepest wounds from the inside out. Even when masked by self-destructive and pleasure-seeking behaviour, our desires will eventually bring us to our knees in surrender, to a higher truth, because our heart is forever guiding us to love ourselves, others and all life unconditionally, even if we hurt ourselves to some degree in the process. In the end, every desire will indeed lead us to wisdom, peace and freedom.

Love has no other desire but to fulfil itself.
Kahlil Gibran

We all want to thrive in a healthy body as a full expression of our true self. I'm sure you'd agree that your deepest desires are always to feel good, to feel love, to feel joy, to feel good enough, to feel peace, to feel safe, to feel inspired, to feel connected, to feel understood, and to feel valued, respected and appreciated for who you truly are. In any moment that *we do not feel these qualities* in our life experience, it is a clear indication that we need to value ourselves more, follow our heart and be more honest in some aspect of our lives. Any time that we feel unhappy, insecure, fearful, lacking, frustrated, guilty, ashamed, lonely or unwell, our soul is crying out for us to be true to ourselves and to focus on what makes us feel alive.

It's clear that the primary reason we do not follow our heart all the time is because of who and what we fear. But even when we have doubts and concerns, our heart will never stop directing us towards where we're meant to be and what we're meant to be doing. We all fear the unknown territories we're being guided into, because moving forward requires us to change and grow beyond our current comfort zone. Ironically, many of us even fear experiencing life in positive ways because we've never known any better or any different. Subconsciously, we actually fear being healthy and happy on a regular basis, because consistently feeling well is not only such a foreign experience, but it can also mirror back to other people how unhappy they are, which then brings up guilt for us.

Sometimes we fear feeling guilt about letting go of a job or a relationship that does not feel good or reflect what we truly want any longer. Sometimes we feel guilt for simply wanting to do something we need to on a particular day, when others have their own expectations of us or are struggling in themselves. Other times we fear the grief that comes with loss or the pain of feeling alone in the world. Quite often, we fear hurting other people when we make a decision to be true to ourselves and follow our heart's inner guidance because sometimes the direction of our growth takes us away from people who are, or have been, very important to us. Beneath these fears, however, it's crucial to know that our deeper fear involves feeling the emotional pain that we ourselves have created in the past when we have abandoned ourselves and betrayed our inner truth.

Rather than face these emotions as they arise within us, many of us just stay in the situations and relationships that we're not happy in because we're either not prepared to take responsibility for what we're really feeling or we don't know how to. We tend to keep pleasing those around us to avoid feeling guilty or to avoid criticism from those who hold unhealthy expectations of us. It is so important to understand that when we fear hurting another, we're most often just afraid of facing what will arise within us once we actually address whatever doesn't feel good or authentic at a particular point in our lives. Our fears arise within us, and then our mind kicks in to justify and rationalize why we should stay where we're miserable, ultimately just to avoid facing the implications of choosing to be honest. Out of habit we reject our true feelings to maintain a sense of control over every aspect of our lives.

Whatever course you decide upon, there is always someone to tell you that you are wrong. There are always difficulties arising which tempt you to believe that your critics are right. To map out a course of action and follow it to an end requires courage.

Ralph Waldo Emerson

One of the biggest obstacles to following our heart is our fear of how others will judge us or what they will think of us. When we react in this way we allow our fears to control our lives and we end up destroying ourselves. Our fear-based thoughts and habits lead us to perceive ourselves as victims who feel sorry for ourselves, when in reality we're simply not being honest with our words and actions here in the present. What we often fail to realize is that trying to please everyone around us all the time is the quickest path to depression, resentment and disease. By continuing to reject ourselves and fear the judgement of others, we create tremendous suffering on top of the pain we're already trying to free ourselves from. What other people think of us and how others judge us or react to us is not really our responsibility. As long as we're being honest and kind when we express our feelings, needs and desires, what we do with our lives is up to us and no one else.

It's very liberating to know that the only reason another person would ever judge us in the first place is because they judge themselves. And the only reason they judge themselves is because they do not feel good about something in their own lives. Through judging us they unconsciously protect themselves from whatever remains unhealed and unloved within them. So whenever you feel judged, or fear being judged, all you have to do is be true to yourself and keep in mind that other people's judgements are not actually personal. As we master loving ourselves unconditionally we also master following our heart without worrying about or fearing what other people will think. When we truly respect the heartfelt force deep within us, we not only respect ourselves more for it, but we also realize that denying its guidance just creates lies and unhappiness. We eventually understand that our own self-judgements and fears are the only obstacles holding us back and everything else is just another excuse to complain or play the victim. When we stop judging ourselves and finally break through our fears, we don't attract judgement from others nearly as much and, when we do, we're simply too busy enjoying our lives to lose energy to it.

Tied up with our fear of being judged is also our fear of failure. We deny the voice of our heart so often because we're afraid of making the 'wrong' decision or of changing our mind somewhere along the way. *What will they think of me? What if I do not or cannot follow through? What if I decide I want or like something different? What if I'm not good enough, smart enough or strong enough?* Even if we fear failing at something, we will always feel better for trying, regardless of the outcome. The true failure is in not trying at all, in not going after what we want and love with all of our heart and soul.

All men dream: but not equally. Those who dream by night in the dusty recesses of their minds wake in the day to find that it was only vanity: but the dreamers of the day are dangerous men, for they may act on their dreams with open eyes and make them their reality.

Thomas E Lawrence

In the end, success is not defined by achieving a goal; it's defined by the courage and strength we find within ourselves, which then leads to inner peace, fulfilment and self-respect. Through following our heart each day, we naturally build belief in ourselves, because the more consistently we honour our inner guidance, the more we trust it is leading us where we're meant to go. This process organically deepens our self-confidence, which just snowballs with every step we take towards authentically enjoying our life.

Personally, I have found that following my heart in the present is how I keep my finger on the pulse of the universe, which never steers me wrong. From this perspective, we cannot make a wrong decision, because every time we follow our heart we experience exactly what we need to experience for our growth and evolution. If we find ourselves desiring something different at any point, there's absolutely nothing wrong with choosing a new direction, because as we become more aware we also become clearer about what we want, need and value. It is always better to take the risk, to jump, to try, to learn and to grow than it is to become paralyzed by who and what we fear. It is always better to be honest and to live, explore and love than to suffer silently with regret. Life is not really about where we end up anyway; it is about how fully and authentically we live each moment and each day. It's about how much and how well we love. If we achieve a goal but have betrayed our inner truth anywhere along the way, we will never *feel the success or self-respect* we're looking for. We can only succeed in life when we follow our heart and therefore know, in every cell of our body, that we've been true to ourselves and to others. When our lives are built upon the inner success that is born from loving ourselves and living with integrity, we not only free ourselves from our suffering, we also discover that the foundations of our daily existence have become so strong that we'll never fear failing in anything our heart inspires us towards ever again.

Practical Questions

In your heart, what do you want and need right now?

What do you want to feel, experience, create, do
and accomplish?

Who or what are you allowing to stop you?

Who or what are you afraid of? Whose judgement do you fear?

Whose approval do you self-destructively seek?

What stories are you telling yourself that are really just
excuses to mask your fear of failure, fear of judgement or fear
of feeling emotional pain?

Are you ready to move beyond your stories and your fears?

If not today, then when will you?

Do you want to live a life that is defined by regret?

Key Affirmations

When I follow my heart, everything always works
out for the best.

The desires in my heart are God and the universe
guiding me forward.

I create all that I desire with ease.

My heart is one with God's heart.

My heart is one with every human heart.

Love is my ultimate desire.

As I follow my heart, I heal my heart and find the love I'm seeking.

What other people think of me is not my concern.

I have all that I need within me to create a fulfilling life that I love.

I am the only person who can give myself permission
to be happy.

CHAPTER 21

Release Your Fear

Our deepest fear is not that we are inadequate. Our deepest fear is that we are powerful beyond measure. It is our light, not our darkness that most frightens us. We ask ourselves, who am I to be brilliant, gorgeous, talented and fabulous? Actually, who are you not to be? You are a child of God. Your playing small doesn't serve the world. There is nothing enlightened about shrinking so that other people won't feel insecure around you. We were born to make manifest the glory of God that is within us. It is not just in some of us: it's in everyone. And when we let our own light shine, we unconsciously give other people permission to do the same. As we are liberated from our own fear, our presence automatically liberates others.

Marianne Williamson

Wherever you are, please take a few slow, deep breaths into your belly. Feel your whole body, from your feet all the way up to the crown of your head, and then down to your fingertips. Please relax any tension you feel and let yourself be. Using each inhalation to open your body and create inner space, welcome everything you're thinking, feeling and experiencing here in this moment. Please be present to your body and your breath.

In the same way that no person wants to be unhappy or unwell, no human being wants to live in fear. If you do not address your underlying fears directly, you will constantly project them onto your ideas of the future, which then causes you to create a life that is defined by what you fear rather than what you love. Fear that is not honestly faced and transformed today will always drive us to think, speak and act in ways that bring about the exact situations and experiences we fear most. When we allow this to continue without being aware of it, we keep reaffirming our limiting beliefs while we simultaneously destroy our health, happiness and everything else potentially positive in our lives.

By paying particular attention to who and what we fear now, we can question why we're scared and begin to see through the thoughts and emotions that are holding us back, making us sick or keeping us unhappy. As we do this we naturally come to understand that our current fears have their roots in the past and we can stop ourselves from unintentionally expecting the same negative or painful events to occur. As we become more aware of our fear-based thinking, we can see how our unresolved experiences from the past shape and limit what we believe our experiences of the future can and will be. The hurt in our heart now and the fear of getting hurt again lead to negative expectations of what is to come. But by bringing more awareness to our fear-based thoughts and habits in the present, we can change this and stop limiting the amazing opportunities each new day presents.

Through learning how to process our fears as they arise, we can release them and drop our expectations of experiencing what we fear. This is also how we let go of the belief that the future will be as hard as the past, which then unlocks more space and energy to enjoy our lives today.

The cave you fear to enter holds the treasure you seek.

Joseph Campbell

Practically speaking, there are two main ways to transform the fear inside of you. Both of these approaches depend first upon you being honest with yourself here in the present rather than running from what you fear through thinking about the future or through making yourself busy in the hope of distracting yourself from the truth.

1. **The first way to transform your fears is to get them out by writing about them or by talking about them with a trusted person in your life.** We do not often share our deepest fears with anyone, because we either deny that they exist or judge ourselves for feeling scared. When we judge ourselves for having fears, most of us then project our own judgement of ourselves out on to others, which leads us to fear being judged by other people. Whether we deny our fears or judge ourselves for having them, they then remain trapped within us, subconsciously

driving our choices in every moment and creating additional suffering. Anything inside of ourselves that we resist will always persist and grow in the shadows of our body and subconscious mind. Through avoiding our fears, they do not go away. Rather they expand in power and destructive influence. As we begin to write about our fears or express them to someone we feel safe talking to, we begin to see through them and thus free the life-force energy that has become trapped in the ongoing loop of fear within us. Honestly expressing our fears immediately breaks this cycle and allows us to reclaim our energy from the destructive pattern of pretending to feel other than we do.

2. **The second way to transform your fear is to focus on love – intentionally to choose love as much as possible every day.** Focusing our thoughts, actions and spoken words on love is an overlooked key to being happy and well. We focus a lot of time and mental energy on the things in our lives that we do not love, or that we fear, and in so doing we unintentionally cause these things to grow. When we train our mind to focus on who we love, what we love and what we love to do, we are focusing our energy on what makes us feel alive and well. What we focus on grows in the same way that what we resist persists. So focusing on what we love feeds energy into the manifestation of more experiences that we enjoy. Even though experiencing more of what we do not want or more of what we fear is the last thing anyone would consciously choose, many of us are trapped in this self-destructive pattern because we don't know anything different. But now that you do understand this process, you can find a way to express

your fears and you can choose to focus on what you love as much as possible each day.

The contrast in our experience between feeling good and feeling fear is always teaching us what we need to know to face and overcome our fear, ultimately so we can enjoy our life and unlock our full capacity to love. Without experiencing fear, we could not know just how liberating the experience of loving ourselves, loving others and loving life truly is. Seen in this light, our fears are actually gifts that challenge us to find the courage and strength to be true to ourselves no matter what. Ironically, our greatest fears always become the bridge to our freedom and joy. They always end up strengthening our commitment to our destiny and our integrity, because they consistently teach us to choose love over fear, which is the only way to create a beautiful life that is full of honesty, peace, health, happiness and deep heart-to-heart connection.

CHAPTER 22

Healthy Self-Esteem, Confidence and Trust in Life

As soon as you trust yourself, you will know how to live.

Johann Wolfgang von Goethe

Wherever you are, please take a few slow, deep breaths into your belly. Feel your whole body, from your feet all the way up to the crown of your head, and then down to your fingertips. Please relax any tension you feel and let yourself be. Using each inhalation to open your body and create inner space, welcome everything you're thinking, feeling and experiencing here in this moment. Please be present to your body and your breath.

If your supposed best friend or your intimate partner continuously betrayed you, day in and day out for years, would you trust them? Of course not, and this is precisely why you do not trust yourself. The criticism, judgement, aggression, betrayal and harm you give yourself is the root cause of weak self-confidence, low self-esteem and a lack of faith in life, the universe and God. The primary reason so many of us do not have faith in ourselves, in our life's purpose, in life itself, in the universe or in God right now is because we know that in the past we have not related to ourselves from a place of unconditional love, kindness and honesty. Rather, we know we've hurt ourselves by lying to ourselves, compromising ourselves, abandoning ourselves, not valuing ourselves, and by not expressing our truth. Most of us do not trust ourselves because we keep betraying ourselves on a daily basis out of fear. We keep giving away our personal power, happiness and security to other people in exchange for their conditional and often toxic love, acceptance, approval and support.

Ideally, we are meant to be our own best friends, but when we betray and hurt ourselves so often we make it quite difficult for us to trust ourselves. As we've seen, our relationship to ourselves is what determines how we perceive and relate to the outer world. So when we feel distrust for life, the universe or God, it's really a symptom of the fact that we do not trust ourselves to be kind, honest and respectful of our true feelings, needs and desires. This is also why using affirmations like 'I love myself' or 'I believe in myself' often do not feel effective or true. We're aware of the fact that we've been horrible to ourselves, and if we're still not treating ourselves well, then of course we won't believe that we're lovable or capable.

The only way to reignite our trust in ourselves and thus our faith in life itself, the universe and God is to commit to being true to ourselves and honest with others in every situation. I've found that we're all born with an inherent faith that cannot be broken or taken away. It's like a seed of knowing and confidence within us that is just waiting to blossom and fill our being and our life. Once we stop compromising ourselves for other people's love, acceptance, approval and support, both our belief in ourselves and our self-esteem naturally strengthen, which leads us to remember that we've both chosen and created all our life experiences to awaken the love, peace and joy within us fully. As we learn to stop betraying ourselves, we're then free to give ourselves the loving attention and care we need for the faith within us to expand infinitely. Eventually, through this process the seeds of clarity, certainty and confidence burst wide open and fill our heart and mind. Through being true to ourselves with each word and action, we finally remember that everything is, always has been and always will be perfect just the way it is. Including ourselves.

> *I have been away from my own soul too long,*
>   *so late sleeping,*
> *But that dove's crying woke me and made me cry.*
> *Praise to all early waking grievers!*
> *Some go first, and others come long afterward.*
> *God blesses all in time ... how to say this to one*
>   *who denies it?*
> *We are all made of the sky's cloth, and everything*
>   *is soul and flowering.*
> *Everything is soul and flowering.*
> *Everything is soul and flowering!*

Jalaluddin Rumi

The trust we have in ourselves, in our life's purpose, in life itself, in the universe and in God are tested every day. We are constantly called to follow the voice of our heart and to break through fear, doubt and our self-imposed limitations. Our rational mind may say, 'But how can that work out?' or 'That's what I want and need, but I don't think it's possible,' or 'I don't deserve that.' But even in these moments, a part of us still knows that it's possible to do, have, create and experience what we desire most in life. Deep down, our true self knows the love inside of us is strong enough to break through every internal and external barrier to enjoying life.

Our lives would be significantly easier if we had learned that there is a fundamental perfection that permeates all of nature and the entire universe. We would all be able to accept ourselves, stop living in fear and thus be completely at peace, if we truly knew that everything is always as it's meant to be, even if we do not fully understand it or like it. If we cannot see and feel this perfection unfolding within our lives right now, it's only because we're still betraying ourselves somehow. And, as a result, we have not healed or understood the emotional pain that still lives beneath our fears and limiting beliefs. This emotional pain is really the only obstacle that blocks the unshakeable trust that's already alive within each of us. Personally, I've found the most empowering perspective to be one where we view life now as though we have selfishly created our lives to one day learn how to enjoy each day fully in a healthy way. This also entails the view that one hundred per cent of our unhappiness, anxiety and sickness stems from all of the times we have not related to ourselves with acceptance, kindness and respect, but rather have let ourselves down.

Seen in this light, any struggle that is present in our lives today is in fact the exact obstacle we need to face and transform in order to heal and move forward in fulfilling our life's purpose. The lessons around loving ourselves unconditionally that we're here to master are present within the aspects of our lives that we're currently not at peace, happy or satisfied with. Once we accept that everything is always exactly as it is meant to be, we can allow ourselves to trust that we're exactly where we need to be, doing exactly what we need to be doing, in order to master the lessons necessary to overcome fear, guilt, shame and insecurity. We were never taught that our lives are embraced by a larger, universal story that is much bigger than our individual lives. However, once we expand our perception on life to include the universe's ever-present perfection, we can finally open to trusting life wholeheartedly *just as it is* without constantly feeling negative or scared about caring for ourselves.

It is very liberating to know that everything that occurs in our lives occurs exactly when it's supposed to, without any exceptions. We overcome fear when we're ready. We stop betraying ourselves when we're ready. We allow ourselves to enjoy our life when we're finally ready to give ourselves permission to do so.

Everything that has ever occurred and everything that will ever occur is part of a larger natural order that we must learn to accept and co-operate with if we genuinely want to find lasting peace, health and happiness. In the same way that the seed of a rose bush sprouts roots, grows upward from the ground and eventually flowers in its own perfect time, our own life purpose, healing and freedom unfold exactly as and when we're ready. A butterfly cannot break free from its cocoon until it's strong enough to see the whole process through, in the same way as a human baby generally takes nine months to gestate before its body organs and entire being is ready for its new life in the outer world. We can never force an organic process and truly achieve a positive harmonious outcome, because all life naturally contains an inner awareness or intelligence that knows exactly when it's time to take the next evolutionary step. What we can do now, however, is stop betraying ourselves. Even if we're scared, we can find the courage to speak and act honestly and kindly so that we can learn to trust ourselves again.

Practical Questions

Do you struggle to believe in yourself? If so, why?

Do you struggle to trust yourself? If so, why?

Do you struggle to trust others? If so, who?

Who in your life mirrors back to you your own self-doubt? In other words, who doubts your abilities and capacities?

Where in your life are you betraying yourself? Can you see how this causes you not to trust yourself?

Where in your life are you dishonest with yourself?

Where in your life right now are you being dishonest with other people?

Which situations do you struggle to accept as purposeful and necessary for your healing and growth? Can you see how you have unintentionally created or allowed these situations to develop? Can you forgive yourself?

What do you need help with in your life right now? When you have some space, try writing a letter to the universe or to God asking for support with the situations and relationships in your life that are challenging, confusing, overwhelming or scary.

What can you focus your energy on today that represents you loving and valuing yourself and therefore honouring what you love to do, want to do or need to do?

Key Affirmations

Being honest with myself is the key to my freedom.

Being honest with other people is the path to peace.

I forgive myself for betraying myself.

I forgive myself for betraying others.

I am committed to loving, honouring and valuing myself.

I want to trust myself again.

I must trust myself truly to trust my intuition with other people.

I must be honest with myself to be honest with others.

I must believe in myself before others will believe in me.

My outer world is always a reflection of my inner world.

I am always supported, protected and safe.

Everything is exactly as it is meant to be.

CHAPTER 23

Love Your Body, but Know You Are So Much More

To be beautiful means to be yourself.

You don't need to be accepted by others.

You need to accept yourself.

Thich Nhat Hanh

Wherever you are, please take a few slow, deep breaths into your belly. Feel your whole body, from your feet all the way up to the crown of your head, and then down to your fingertips. Please relax any tension you feel and let yourself be. Using each inhalation to open your body and create inner space, welcome everything you're thinking, feeling and experiencing here in this moment. Please be present to your body and your breath.

Learning to love, care for and accept our physical body is undoubtedly a key to finding peace and enjoying our life, especially because so many of us struggle with physical insecurity, judgement and criticism. Our perception of our physical appearance is often a primary influence that determines what we think and how we feel about ourselves more than anything else in life. Unfortunately, we never really learned that while who we are includes our physical body, we are in fact far greater than what we see when we look in the mirror. As we learn how to love ourselves unconditionally on a non-physical level, we start to remember and identify with our ever-present inner beauty, which is never lacking or deficient in any way. But until we reach a place where we can see both our value and the miraculous truth of our life, many of us are constantly fixated on trying to look different from the way we currently do, and this constant state of non-acceptance is at the heart of much of our suffering.

In my experience, anything about our physical body that we do not accept completely is a reflection of something deeper within us that we have not learned to embrace or respect. Anything we perceive to be a physical imperfection or insecurity is merely a symptom, or a cry from our soul, asking us to accept and value some aspect of our non-physical being more fully. One of the most empowering insights I've discovered on this topic is that when we live in a way where our emotions, needs and desires do not matter to us, we then feel they do not matter to those around us either, and this causes us to feel 'we' ourselves do not matter. The result of this dynamic is a sentiment that says, *'Why would I want to care for or accept my body if I do not matter? If my life does not feel good, and I do not feel good in my body, then why would I want to take care of the body that is the vehicle for this life?'*

Because most of us learned to reject our feelings, needs and dreams growing up, we set up a relationship to our inner world that said these inner truths are worthless and do not matter. But these non-physical dynamics are a vital part of who we are and they must be valued for us to feel we have intrinsic value and worth. Our physical insecurities are actually rooted in our mental and emotional insecurities, which are the true cause of our physical self-rejection and criticism. Our lack of acceptance emotionally becomes physical rejection, judgement and criticism, because when we make ourselves wrong emotionally we do not feel good inside our body, and the result is not feeling good about our body. If we struggle to accept our thoughts and emotions, we will always struggle to accept our physical self. Similarly, if we don't care for our heart and feel that our emotions, needs and dreams matter, we end up criticizing ourselves for not finding the courage to live authentically and this stops us from feeling genuine care for our body.

What's the point of trying to keep our body as healthy as possible if we don't enjoy being alive?

From this perspective it should be very clear as to why so many of us struggle to implement the healthy lifestyle habits that support our optimal physical wellbeing. It's hard to find the inspiration and commitment to care for our body when we feel unworthy of love in our heart. At the other end of the spectrum, hopefully it's also clear why those people who do force themselves to focus on their physical body, but do not go deeper into valuing themselves emotionally, are often quite unhappy or lonely. Sometimes a person who exercises regularly and eats very healthily can be just as insecure as someone who does not. Regardless, in both cases, we're all guilty of not valuing our true feelings sometimes, either because we never learned how to or because we're scared of being vulnerable. When we're being hard on ourselves and critical, it's because we're still not honouring or listening to our deeper non-physical self.

> *The most beautiful people we have known are those who*
> *have known defeat, known suffering, known struggle,*
> *known loss, and have found their way out of the depths.*
> *These persons have an appreciation, a sensitivity, and*
> *an understanding of life that fills them with compassion,*
> *gentleness, and a deep loving concern. Beautiful people*
> *do not just happen.*
>
> **Elisabeth Kübler-Ross**

Most of us identify solely with the reflection of ourselves that we see when we look in a mirror, but when we truly stop to consider and feel whether or not we are merely our physical body, the logical conclusion, to some degree, will always end up being 'no'. The truth is that our physical body is an energetic expression of our non-physical self in the same way that our thoughts and emotions are also energetic expressions of our larger and deeper soul. Just as branches, leaves and fruit are natural expressions that grow from the trunk, or core, of a fruit-bearing tree, so too are our thoughts, emotions and physical body natural expressions of a much deeper consciousness at the heart of who we are.

Who we truly are is actually a field of vibrant energy, where the atoms that make up our physical and non-physical self are united with all life, nature and the entire universe. Even if we're not aware of this, the truth remains that our non-physical self is what fills, shapes and drives both the structure of our physical body as well as its life-giving functions. Our relationship to and perception of our physical body was 'shaped' by the unique familial, educational, cultural and media influences that we encountered throughout our early life. However, underneath all of the limiting beliefs we might now hold in relation to our physical appearance, we will always find internalized emotion from past experiences that we have not processed.

As we've seen in previous chapters, the insecurity, unhappiness and dissatisfaction within us will always lead us back to the situations where we have not related to ourselves with kindness, honesty and courage, either because we didn't know how to or because we were afraid to. This internal dynamic always leads us to judge ourselves and judge our physical body in order to protect ourselves from feeling the unhealed emotions that are still stored within us. Regardless of why, how or what we judge about our physical body, we're either completely identified with our body image, which will always be unhealthy for us, or we're just attached to limiting beliefs about our appearance that definitely do not reflect our whole true self.

Whether we judge ourselves as being overweight or underweight, too small or too big in some part of our body, unattractive, imperfect or disabled in any way, the truth is that, when growing up, we learned a very limiting view of ourselves that does not honour our non-physical self. We all need to wake up and realize that feeling good inside is always the key to feeling good physically. This dynamic is also true for every form of addiction that influences how we look and feel physically. Whether we're addicted to food, alcohol, cigarettes, drugs, sex, money, attention, misery or being sick, underneath all our self-destructive habits there's simply internalized emotion that we're running from and subconsciously protecting ourselves from feeling. Again, when we feel we do not matter, that our feelings, needs and desires have no value or worth, we find things with which to numb ourselves or use self-destructive substances briefly to feel better, which only lead to more physical symptoms for us to feel bad about.

The key to accepting our physical body is to stop running and face the underlying emotions that are (1) causing us to judge our physical body, (2) causing us to abuse our physical body, and (3) creating the physical symptoms that we're experiencing. As we heal the emotions we've repressed and we learn to be true to ourselves in every situation, we finally start to feel that we matter and that both our physical and non-physical self have value, which then guides us to care for and speak to our body with kindness all the time. As we create a life that is both meaningful and true to our deeper values, we then feel much better internally and we're naturally inspired towards a healthier lifestyle. As we've explored earlier, being authentic now is how we heal our emotional insecurities and develop more self-respect and self-worth. This process of emotional self-acceptance then supports us to feel better about ourselves each day, which snowballs into further habits that support our overall happiness and sense of wellbeing. When we're finally ready to surrender our inner fight and wholeheartedly accept the truth as we feel it, we open the door to heal both our physical self-judgements and the underlying emotional rejection, which then clears the way to intentionally create and achieve whatever we want or need to look and feel great.

Nothing ever goes away until it teaches us what we need to know.

Pema Chodron

Every physical judgement, criticism and insecurity comes back to our need and desire for love. Having grown up around people who did not love and accept themselves unconditionally, most of us did not learn how to care for ourselves in healthy ways. Rather, we inherited multiple forms of self-sabotage genetically and emotionally from our parents, because they could not help but pass on their unhealed dysfunctions. For example, if one of our parents struggled to feel beautiful, then we were most likely born with the same limiting perception of ourselves already activated within our consciousness. Likewise, if we had parents who were very hard on themselves, then they were most likely just as hard on us. This makes it easy to see how over time most of us just end up internalizing our parents' criticism and judgement and literally walk around with their voices in our head.

Underneath every physical self-judgement, self-criticism and insecurity we will always find emotional pain that was first inherited and then built upon very early in our lives through our learned self-harm. It's liberating to know that so many of us feel as though *we were just born feeling insecure, unlovable, inadequate, imperfect or unattractive*, because this form of suffering and self-destruction was still active in our parents at the time of our conception and was unknowingly passed down. This is why it's so important to break the cycle now in ourselves, so we don't perpetuate so much pain and struggle for future generations.

The underlying negativity we all have to overcome is the result of (1) emotions and beliefs that we absorbed in our mother's womb between our conception and our birth, (2) us not knowing how to express our emotions as children, (3) our parents not loving themselves unconditionally, (4) our parents not being able to love us unconditionally, (5) our current patterns around repressing what we feel, and (6) from a spiritual perspective, our soul's karma and core lessons in this lifetime. Fortunately, no one has to live feeling negative about him or herself physically forever because through loving ourselves now we can transform all of the inner obstacles to feeling good about ourselves. The degree to which we experience the positive feelings we crave depends upon how honestly we're willing to face ourselves and our lives. If we're prepared to be true to ourselves in the present, no matter what, there is nothing that is outside our power to transform. With patience and commitment, each of us can take full responsibility for caring for our body each day, and for living a healthy, balanced and proactive lifestyle while we heal our emotional wounds and intentionally re-create our lives.

Settling for a lack of care or acceptance for our physical body is often symptomatic of us just waiting to be loved unconditionally by someone else. It's an unconscious expectation to be accepted, reassured and supported in the ways we were not as children. It's healthy to know that it will never matter how much another person loves or accepts us if we do not embrace ourselves fully from the inside out. Being appreciated by another person helps, but each of us must eventually realize that we are the person whose love we've been waiting for. At some point, in our own heart and mind, we have to stop fixating on our perceived imperfections and allow ourselves to enjoy life. Through following your heart, speaking your truth, focusing on whatever makes you feel well, and engaging in situations where you feel like your true self, you will eventually overcome the limitation of being identified with your physical body or any particular aspect of it. Once you face the emotional truth you've been rejecting, the deeper truth that both your body and life are a miracle will override any remaining self-criticism or insecurity that arises.

Practical Questions

What do you struggle to love or like about your physical body?

What are you insecure about physically?

Can you feel that you are so much more than just your physical body? Can you feel the life-force energy vibrating within you?

If you look into your eyes in the mirror can you see that you are much greater than just your physical body?

What are you waiting for (if *waiting* metaphorically equals 'carrying extra physical weight') to go after what you want and love? What are you waiting for finally to be true to yourself? Whose love, understanding, approval, acceptance or support are you waiting for? What if you never get it?

If you overeat, can you see how you're numbing yourself to uncomfortable emotions? Can you see how you're seeking pleasure in unhealthy ways because you're stopping yourself from speaking and acting from your truth each day?

If you feel excessively overweight, can you see how subconsciously you've built a physical shell to protect your heart from being hurt?

If you struggle with anorexia, can you see how you are over-identified with your body and looking for love externally?

If you struggle with bulimia, can you see how you are (1) looking for love, joy and pleasure and (2) trying to numb yourself to your emotions?

Are you ready to be happy and love yourself from the inside out?

What did you need to hear as a child about your physical appearance but never heard? If you could tell your younger self anything right now, what would you want him or her to know?

If you think about past experiences in which you felt insecure, unloved or unattractive, what did your younger self need to hear or know to feel good about him or herself in that moment or situation?

If you could go back in time and stick up for yourself as a child, what would you say and to whom would you say it?

Are you ready to commit to caring for your body? Are you ready to make lifestyle choices that are free of guilt? Are you ready to eat healthily, exercise regularly and express your emotions, needs and desires honestly?

Key Affirmations

It's okay for me to feel beautiful.

[Your name], you are beautiful just as you are.

I love and appreciate my body for supporting me and my life.

I am not just my body. I am so much more.

Thank you, body. Thank you, bones. Thank you, organs.
Thank you, cells.

Thank you for my healthy, flexible, beautiful body.

Thank you for my strong immune system. Thank you for my
strong digestive system. Thank you for my strong circulatory
system. Thank you for my strong reproductive system.

I accept my body as it is, and I commit to caring for
my body's health daily.

My body is a temple for my soul. It is my temporary home.

I am one with the infinite universe.

I am a cell in the universe's body.

My true self is eternal and immortal. I was never born and
I will never die.

Genuinely to care for my body, I must genuinely
care for my heart.

My true feelings, needs and desires must matter to me if I want
my body to matter in a healthy way.

Additional Self-Love Body Practice

Speaking to your body with love, kindness and positivity on a regular basis can help you replace your negative thoughts and self-judgements. Many of my clients (both male and female) have found it helpful to use the affirmations opposite while moisturizing their entire body either after showering or after bathing. Even if it's challenging at first, and even if you do not believe what you're saying completely, please be patient with yourself and persist, because in time you will allow yourself to open and receive your own loving support.

CHAPTER 24

Practical Nutrition and Lifestyle Guidance

Be careful about reading health books. You may die of a misprint.

Mark Twain

Wherever you are, please take a few slow, deep breaths into your belly. Feel your whole body, from your feet all the way up to the crown of your head, and then down to your fingertips. Please relax any tension you feel and let yourself be. Using each inhalation to open your body and create inner space, welcome everything you're thinking, feeling and experiencing here in this moment. Please be present to your body and your breath.

Considering that there are thousands of books about nutrition, exercise and caring for your body, it's unnecessary for me to go too deeply into the physical aspects of loving your body. I'm sure you're well aware of what this entails. For our purposes, I will briefly share what I've found to be the most important and most effective approaches to loving your body from the perspective of creating a healthy and balanced lifestyle that is based on unconditional self-love. Please keep in mind that all of us are slightly different when it comes to what's best for our body type, inner nature, lifestyle and even the unique climate we live in. Overall, however, there are some key guidelines I've found to be generally supportive for everybody. Having said that, I personally recommend and live by the following physical approaches to unconditional self-love.

- Try to drink a good amount of clean water (at least two to three litres) each day to flush out toxins in your body and to stay hydrated. Try to drink only natural spring or mineral water. There are also numerous filters available that you can buy for your home to filter the water from your taps.
- Try to drink at least two cups of water in the morning

before you eat or drink anything else. This hydrates your cells, wakes up your organs, flushes out toxins, activates your digestive system, and helps your whole body function optimally throughout the day.

- Try to eat unprocessed, organic whole foods as much as possible: whole foods such as vegetables, fruits, legumes and whole grains, and, for those who need or choose to, lean meats and wild freshwater or saltwater fish (as opposed to farm-raised). Once again, everybody is unique, so you have to find the combinations that work best for you.
- Try to avoid genetically modified foods (GMOs).
- Also try to avoid foods containing preservatives, artificial colourings and artificial sweeteners.
- Find a high-quality daily multivitamin from your local alternative healthcare practitioner. Other nutritional supplements that are generally great for all people to take daily, no matter what their age or state of health, include high-grade fish oils or high-quality plant oils with omega 3, 6 and 9 fatty acids, probiotics, and some form of green superfood, such as spirulina or blue-green algae.
- Try to avoid eating large amounts of processed flour in bread, pasta, cereals, pastries and cakes. Homemade bread and pasta are better for us, if you love having these in your diet.
- Try to avoid eating fast food and processed meat.
- Try to avoid eating too much dairy in the form of milk and cheese, because these foods create phlegm, stagnation and blockages in our body and energy system. They also decrease mental clarity and sharpness.
- Try to avoid eating too much sugar in the form of candy, soft drinks and processed juices.

An American monkey, after getting drunk on brandy,
would never touch it again, and thus is much wiser than
most men.

Charles Darwin

- Try to avoid drinking too much alcohol.
- Try to avoid smoking completely.
- Try to avoid prescription and recreational drugs.
- Try to exercise in some way each day, even if that means taking a few short walks around your neighbourhood or block. Walking, running, hiking, cycling, yoga, qi gong, tai chi, weightlifting, dancing and swimming are all great ways to move your body, blood and energy to keep yourself strong and well. Find something active that you enjoy and do it regularly.
- Considering the last point, although housework undoubtedly requires a lot of energy, it is not the same as taking time specifically to focus on loving yourself and caring for your physical health.
- Sexual intimacy is very important for most people. If you have not chosen a life of celibacy for religious or spiritual reasons, then regular sexual intimacy is healthy for your body, heart and soul. Bringing a great deal of presence, awareness, communication and respect to this part of our lives is also very important in our overall healing and spiritual awakening.
- Take time just to *be*, especially out in nature when possible. Meditation, reading, writing in a journal, taking a bath, listening to music or making yourself a cup of tea are all great ways to slow down. Allow yourself time and space simply to be without having to do anything, please anyone or be anywhere.

- Try to get between seven and nine hours of good sleep each night.
- With that in mind, if you're a coffee drinker, try not to have coffee within five hours of going to bed.
- Try to respect yourself when you dress for your day. Whether you're going to work, out with friends, family or your partner, how you dress does affect how you feel. Wear clothes that truly make you feel good about yourself.
- Many deodorants and toothpastes contain chemicals called parabens or aluminium, which are horrible for our health. Please find a natural deodorant and toothpaste to use daily.
- Also, a number of shampoos, conditioners and other body-care products are full of chemicals that are not good for our health. Some to avoid are sodium lauryl sulphate, sodium laureth sulphate, propylene glycol, triethanolamine, pesticides, fluoride, lead, methyl mercury, BPA, bisphenols, phthalates, BHT, phenoxyethanol, fragrance, organophosphates, dioxins, DDT, diethylstilboestrol, PCB, mercury, glycol ethers, homosalate, phosphates, phemaldahyde, chlorine, SLS, methyl mercury, triclosan, methylisothiazolinone, sodium fluoride, octocrylene, cocamide DEA and diazolidinyl urea.

The greatest of follies is to sacrifice health for any other kind of happiness.

Arthur Schopenhauer

When considering the above-mentioned approaches to caring for your body, please remember that moderation is always the best approach. Even moderation in being moderate is healthy once in a while too. The 'middle way' tends to be optimal, as extremes of any kind throw us out of balance and often snap back with equal force the opposite way. Please also remember that being kind towards yourself, regardless of your nutritional and lifestyle choices, is the top priority. If it takes you a while truly to love your body and relate to your body with love, then so be it. There's no need to create more suffering. Life is too short. At the same time, your level of health is yours to enjoy or not. It is your choice.

CHAPTER 25

Loving Yourself Within a Relationship

My primary relationship is with myself – all others are mirrors of it. As I learn to love myself, I automatically receive the love and appreciation that I desire from others. If I am committed to myself and to living my truth, I will attract others with equal commitment. My willingness to be intimate with my own deep feelings creates the space for intimacy with another. As I learn to love myself, I receive the love I desire from others.

Shakti Gawain

Wherever you are, please take a few slow, deep breaths into your belly. Feel your whole body, from your feet all the way up to the crown of your head, and then down to your fingertips. Please relax any tension you feel and let yourself be. Using each inhalation to open your body and create inner space, welcome everything you're thinking, feeling and experiencing here in this moment. Please be present to your body and your breath.

Developing healthy, loving and supportive relationships is one of the most important ingredients for living a happy and fulfilling life. But today many of us place more value on things like achieving worldly success, always being right, making money or projecting a certain image of ourselves out into the world. In focusing on these apparently easier aspects of life over and above our precious personal relationships, we not only avoid our most important life lessons, we also pass up some of the deepest heartfelt and soul-nourishing experiences available to us as human beings. Although our personal relationships can be challenging, they offer priceless opportunities for the healing and growth we all eventually learn to value. Regardless of the external form a relationship takes, we always come together with other people to learn about love, kindness and compassion, to become more honest, to heal past wounds and, ultimately, to master loving ourselves unconditionally so that we can unlock more of our capacity to love others in pure and healthy ways.

Each relationship in our life right now is meant to help us transform our limiting beliefs and bring down the walls surrounding our heart. When we're triggered and reacting, our relationships are mirroring back to us the hurt, fear, insecurity, anger, guilt and shame that are stored inside our body and which separate us from the honesty, kindness, understanding and joy we want to share with others. Eventually we realize that we cannot and do not heal alone. We do not exist in isolation even when we feel lonely. Since most of our current struggles have their roots in habits we developed in reaction to our early relationships, we have attracted the people around us today to show us both what really matters in life as well as how or where we do not matter to ourselves fully yet. Not only do the people in our life expose our limiting beliefs and unhealed emotional pain, but they also inspire and bring forth the love within us more powerfully than any other aspect of our lives. However, along with the flowering of this love we feel for others, the aspects of ourselves we're still rejecting arise to be transformed, because the love within us forces out whatever needs to be healed. As challenging as some of our relationships can be, the people who test us the most are our greatest teachers. They teach us to forgive, to keep our heart open, to see through other people's reactions and to value ourselves in every moment. Paradoxically, since most of us grew up around very unhealthy forms of relationship, which then contributed to the creation of an unhealthy relationship to ourselves, often we need to take space from our close relationships in order to think clearly and to create a healthy relationship with ourselves.

Self-love is the foundation of our loving practice. Without it our other efforts to love fail. Giving ourselves love we provide our inner being with the opportunity to have the unconditional love we may have always longed to receive from someone else.

Bell Hooks

It can be hard to view our relationships in a positive light because our close relationships have often been, or still are, very painful. Although it may be difficult to accept, our current relationships can only ever be as healthy as our relationship is with ourselves. In many cases, our close relationships reveal the aggressive, critical, insecure, judgemental and self-destructive relationship that many of us have maintained with ourselves. In other words, the amount of love, respect, kindness, appreciation and happiness that we experience in our interactions with other people is a direct reflection of the amount of love, respect, kindness, appreciation and happiness that we currently feel within and towards ourselves.

From this perspective, each person in our lives reflects back to us an aspect of ourselves that we're being called to value, embrace or be honest about. This is demonstrated by the fact that if we do not accept, appreciate, respect or believe in ourselves, then most of the people in our lives will not do so either. As we learn to value, express and care for ourselves each day, however, we eventually find that the people in our lives will reflect back the loving respect we've cultivated for ourselves. We also find that who we are and what we embody inspires others to do the same. This process can initially trigger reactions in the people around us, especially those who are accustomed to us pleasing them. But over time, our honesty and love for ourselves gives them permission to be honest and loving towards themselves as well. Once the dust of reaction and manipulation settles, the people we can have a healthy relationship with will naturally remain in our lives.

Although it can be tough to see at times, the process of learning to love and value ourselves fully within our close relationships entails realizing that other people can only bring up feelings within us to the degree that we react to their behaviour or words. The ultimate truth is that no one can make us feel anything when our sense of self, worth and confidence are strong. Through an honest vulnerability and commitment to self-awareness, we can learn to live in a way where we take full responsibility for our emotions and reactions to other people. Selfishly for our own wellbeing, we eventually need to learn to find the lesson in anything we believe someone is making us feel, but which in reality is being drawn out of us or allowed by us.

If someone's words or actions trigger guilt, fear, insecurity, anger or hurt within us, we have to learn to view these emotions as our responsibility to both attend to and understand – especially if we want to enjoy our relationships and our life. Even, for example, in a situation where we instinctually feel someone could be lying to us, but we begin to feel insecure, it is a huge lesson for us in valuing ourselves to find the courage to address the situation honestly, while also taking responsibility for our insecure reaction at the same time. This is also true for common situations where we feel criticized by another person or when someone tries to make us feel bad for being true to ourselves. Although it can be hard to find clarity around, we attract the exact experiences necessary to draw out feelings like guilt, frustration or self-doubt that need to be healed within us. The only way to trust ourselves completely and thus have an honest healthy relationship with another human being is to stop rejecting ourselves or making our feelings wrong.

If we truly want to enjoy our lives and overcome the suffering created in unhealthy relationships, we're eventually forced to recognize that when we relate to other people, we come either from a place of value and respect for ourselves or from a place of fear, insecurity and inadequacy. When we relate to others from a place of self-worth and respect, we give and relate genuinely from a place of clarity, integrity and peace, which means we do not have an inner conflict occurring as to whether we should or should not give of ourselves in some way. This means we give freely of ourselves without expecting anything in return, without placing conditions on what we give or do, and without manipulating people based on what we've given or done.

Valuing ourselves within our relationships also means we do not act or speak just to please others or to make them happy. It means we do our best daily to be completely honest with ourselves and with whomever we're relating to, even if they want or expect something different or something more from us. When we relate to others from a place of fear, insecurity or inadequacy, we tend to give and relate out of feelings of obligation or out of a fear of losing their love, a fear of hurting them, a fear of being hurt by them or a fear of feeling guilty for saying no. When we come from fear, we act and speak merely to please, and we abandon what we truly feel, which only leads to pain, frustration, anger and resentment.

A large proportion of our suffering is the result of us betraying ourselves in relationship. We all hurt ourselves to some degree while interacting with other people, because this is what we learned from the unhealthy relationships we grew up around. Although by this stage in your life

Pause now to ask yourself if it is worth paying so much for so little. Imagine you say to the person whose special love you want, 'Leave me free to be myself, to think my thoughts, to indulge my tastes, to follow my inclinations, to behave in ways I decide are to my liking.' The moment you say those words you will understand that you are asking for the impossible. To ask to be special to someone means essentially to be bound to the task of making yourself pleasing to this person. And therefore to lose your freedom ... Maybe now you are ready to say, 'I'd rather have my freedom than your love.' If you could either have company in prison or walk the earth in freedom all alone, which would you choose? Now say to this person, 'I leave you free to be yourself, to think your thoughts, to indulge your tastes, to follow your inclinations, and to behave in any way you decide is to your liking.' In saying those words to another, to any other, to your beloved – in saying those words you have set yourself free. You are now ready to love. For when you cling, what you offer another is not love but a chain by which both you and they are bound. Love can only exist in freedom. The true lover seeks only the good of the beloved which requires especially the liberation of the beloved from the lover.

Anthony de Mello, *The Way to Love*

you're probably aware that this needs to change, many of us still falsely believe that if we please others and make others happy then they will please us and make us happy in return. Eventually, however, often after much pain and confusion, we realize that no one can ever truly bring us lasting happiness or fulfilment besides ourselves. We also realize that no matter how much we do for or try to please another person, it will never, finally, be enough to fulfil them or make them happy.

From this perspective, it becomes obvious that what most of us tend to call love is riddled with subtle forms of manipulation and unhealthy compromise. Betraying ourselves to meet the needs of another person, just so that person will love us in return, is not true love. Similarly, expecting someone to compromise him or herself just to satisfy all our personal preferences, merely as a prerequisite to us expressing love or affection towards them, is extremely misguided when it comes to the quality of love that we're all actually looking for. Although we're all just doing the best with what we know, I've found it helpful to be aware that there are much healthier and honest expressions of love available to us when we commit to truly valuing ourselves.

As much as we sometimes think it to be so, the people in our lives do not exist merely to fulfil our own personal needs and desires. Nor do we exist merely to meet their needs and wishes. That was partially our mother's and father's role during our early years; it is not our partner's, our friends' or our children's responsibility now. Each of us is destined to learn how to fulfil our own needs by giving ourselves the loving attention and support we did not receive as children and that we now unconsciously look for from other people. At some point we're all forced to realize that achieving lasting happiness and fulfilment is always dependent upon the quality of love and honesty present within our own relationship to ourselves. If we truly want to create healthy, supportive and conscious relationships that last, we must first create a healthy, supportive and conscious relationship with ourselves. Likewise, if we genuinely want to experience true, unconditional love with another human being, we must first commit to finding the source of true unconditional love within us, which is only possible through being true to ourselves in every moment and situation.

Practical Questions

In which relationships do you struggle to value yourself and thus talk about your true feelings, needs and desires? Why do you feel you struggle with this?

Who in your life do you find it hard to accept as your teacher?

Who do you expect to make you happy, heal you, rescue you, take care of you or fix you?

Who do you try to make happy, please, fix, heal or rescue?

Who do you betray yourself for and expect to do the same in return?

What can you focus your energy on today that represents you valuing yourself and therefore honouring what you love to do, want to do or need to do?

Key Affirmations

My relationships are only as healthy as I am.

My health and happiness are in my own hands.

Deep down I know I want honest relationships that I feel good in.

I want to be loved for who I am, not for what I do or how I please.

Every person in my life is my teacher.

It's never too late to start over.

It's never too late to love again. I'll never be too old for
love and romance.

I deserve intimacy and deep connection.

When I'm healthy and happy in myself, I naturally create healthy
and happy relationships.

I deserve healthy, happy and loving relationships in my life.

Additional Practice for Attracting a Life Partner or Soul Mate

1. Please make a list of all the qualities you would like in a life partner. List all of the character traits as well as all of the physical traits you desire. Then, list everything you would like to do, create, feel and experience with this person. Lastly, list what you value most in life and thus want your partner to value as a priority also.

2. Once the above list is complete, please turn your request into a letter or prayer to the universe or to God and ask for what you want. 'Dear God [or universe], please send me my soul mate who ... Thank you for my soul mate who is ...'

3. Once steps one and two are complete, please close your eyes and imagine what life will look like and feel like when you meet the person you're looking for. Please visualize what you will do, create, feel and experience with this person. Then, in your heart, give thanks to the universe or to God for sending you your teacher, lover and best friend. Although it may seem awkward at first, this is a very effective technique to help you attract what you want.

4. Finally, after completing steps one through three, please focus on taking amazing care of yourself, be patient and be open to whomever you meet. Do what makes you feel most alive, happy and well each day so that you're at peace with yourself and your own life as much as possible before meeting someone. If you can achieve this, then you will not expect your future partner to make you happy. Rather, he or she will be the 'icing on the cake' of a life that is already great.

Additional Practice for Healing Your Current Relationship(s)

If you are struggling with any relationship in your life, whether it's with your partner, spouse, parent, child or friend, it is very helpful to write the person a letter expressing how you feel, what you want and what you need. At first, I recommend you write a draft of the letter – one that you will not give to them – so that you can express yourself fully without holding back. Then, it is helpful to rewrite the letter a second time with more clarity and personal responsibility, and with less reaction and blame.

In your letter(s), I recommend using non-aggressive phrases such as:

- I feel … (hurt, angry, unappreciated, used, loved, respected, valued, etc.)
- I need … (space to be, clear communication, respect, honesty, passion, etc.)
- I want … (to do things I enjoy, have fun, share emotionally, travel, etc.)
- I feel hurt, angry, frustrated or unvalued when …
- I love it when you …
- I appreciate it when you …
- I am not happy in this relationship …
- I need to feel safe, that I can trust you, that I matter, etc. …
- I want to go, do, create, experience, etc. …
- I want us to honour and respect what's important to each other …
- I'd like to be able to …
- It's important to me that …
- I really value or need some 'me' time.

Underneath every situation, in this moment, we all have important feelings, needs and desires that must be valued for us to (1) have a healthy relationship with ourselves, (2) have healthy relationships with others, and (3) be at peace, happy and fulfilled. If we can learn to identify what we feel, need and desire in the present, we can then learn to express ourselves from a place of clarity, love and personal responsibility.

Another extremely helpful approach to healing a relationship with someone close to you is to ask them what they feel, want and need. Often, we do not even know what we're feeling, desiring or needing because we never learned how to be this present or clear with ourselves or with those around us. If you can help the people in your life to understand themselves more deeply in this way, there's nothing that cannot be overcome, healed or harmonized for the benefit of everyone involved.

With the above in mind, when writing your letter(s), you can ask the person you're addressing what he or she feels, wants and needs, in addition to expressing your own position. This particular approach opens a space that will help both you and the other person move forward with peace, understanding and mutual respect.

CHAPTER 26

Healthy Commitment to Self and Other

Set your life on fire. Seek those who fan your flames.

Jalaluddin Rumi

Wherever you are, please take a few slow, deep breaths into your belly. Feel your whole body, from your feet all the way up to the crown of your head, and then down to your fingertips. Please relax any tension you feel and let yourself be. Using each inhalation to open your body and create inner space, welcome everything you're thinking, feeling and experiencing here in this moment. Please be present to your body and your breath.

Before any form of external commitment can begin or remain healthy, we have to commit to being true to ourselves completely. Until we commit to ourselves – to saying our deeper feelings, values, needs and aspirations matter now – our personal and professional commitments will always result in stress, confusion, struggle or heartache, especially our intimate relationships. If you're currently having trouble committing to an intimate relationship, it's important to be kind to yourself as you navigate your next steps. You are feeling this way for a reason. No one wants to feel insecure, fearful, owned, controlled or limited in a partnership. However, it is equally important to become aware of why you feel as you do. For this reason, it's empowering to know that the main reason we struggle with commitment, whether we're starting a new relationship or questioning an existing one, is because we still have not fully committed to ourselves, which ultimately entails learning to value and be true to ourselves in all our interactions. This is a major challenge for all of us, but it's the only road to lasting peace, happiness and freedom – whether we're seeking lasting true love or not.

A relationship cannot be healthy or sustainable if our relationship with ourselves is not healthy and intimately honest. If we have not consciously made a commitment to be true to ourselves on a daily basis, we cannot put or keep two feet in a relationship. Likewise, if we haven't learned to make ourselves happy, then we have a habit of always trying to please others in the hope they will return the favour, which inevitably leads to painful lessons. When we have not learned to enjoy our own company and thus don't value our own space yet, we will fill it with people we feel limited by, solely because we fear being alone, which always results in a vicious cycle of feeling trapped and resentful, while we blame a partner for what we haven't addressed in ourselves.

For these reasons, when we feel we do not have the tools or the experience to both communicate and act upon our true needs, feelings and goals, we'll either avoid all forms of commitment or we'll repeatedly end up in situations that we cannot give ourselves fully to. In both cases we often fear we'll lose ourselves in the relationship, which leads either to a fear of entering any or to a desire to be free from an existing one. If we've learned to please others to our own detriment, in exchange for companionship, love, affection, attention and support, justifiably we are left fearful of hurting ourselves and of allowing ourselves to get hurt.

If we've had our heart broken, or broken another's heart, it can be scary to give ourselves fully to someone or to feel someone giving themselves to us. Both dynamics bring us back to the task of talking about our current feelings, fears, needs, reservations and hopes, so both parties feel all cards are on the table. When one or both parties is able to honour themselves in this way, it symbolizes a healthy commitment to oneself, and the result is always less assumption and more truth, which leads to less pain and more clarity for everyone involved.

Whether a relationship is just starting or is pre-existing, by honouring our instincts now, even if there is a lack of clarity, we stop betraying what we feel and thus avoid attracting further betrayal from others. When we speak to our intuitive gut feelings rather than brushing them under the carpet we also prevent situations where we're perceived as the betrayer. In simple terms, saying yes when we feel no, or saying no when we want to say yes, lead to sadness, hurt and dissatisfaction. Making promises we don't feel completely good about, or asking for a commitment from someone who we know is not ready, are both forms of self-betrayal. They are habits grounded in insecurity and are how we make ourselves the victim of what we fear.

Once we're more practised in speaking and acting based on our truth, we become willing and able to give ourselves fully to an intimate relationship – if this is in fact what we want and what feels good to us. When we finally trust ourselves we can consciously choose to commit to another, because we're confident we will not lose, abandon or hurt ourselves with or for them. Ideally though, we want to feel well, happy and whole without needing someone in our life; then, if we feel nourished, engaged and inspired by someone's presence, we will naturally feel inclined to spend time with them, regardless of where it leads. Similarly, when we're met in this way by another person who's coming from a place of self-awareness and wholeness, they too don't really need us but rather want to share themselves with us. A time may come when this changes though, either because one or both parties begin to feel differently, and if it does, if we truly value ourselves, based on a solid commitment to ourselves, we will know and trust that all is as it's meant to be. Rather than becoming tortured by insecurity and thinking there's something wrong with us, or feeling guilty for being the one who needs a change, we'll accept our feelings and those of the other, trusting we will both be okay. Eventually both parties will find someone else to share their life with if this is what they desire.

Beyond a day-to-day authenticity, our commitments often become habitual and empty. For many people they are inherited social customs, held in place by limiting beliefs, which mask our fears, insecurities and untapped ability to express ourselves. This is why so many people break their promises or end up running from their commitments. They have signed up for something they were not ready for because they did not understand who they are or love themselves yet. Genuine wholehearted commitment is really based on a choice we make each day to be real and respectful, first towards ourselves and then with those we are in relationship to. If we are rejecting or hiding any part of ourself, our external commitments will simply mirror back to us where and how we are abandoning ourselves. These commitments temporarily take us away from the peace, joy and love we're seeking, which are already present now beneath our fears, wounds and the voices in our head. Paradoxically and yet purposefully, we all try to escape ourselves at times through impulsive or excessive external commitments, which eventually force us to come back to and commit to ourselves in a deeper way.

As most of us have now learned the hard way, true love can only exist in freedom. Yet simultaneously we're all looking to share the tremendous amount of love we have in our heart with people who appreciate and respect us. For this reason, it's critical we make a sincere commitment to developing the healthy self-intimacy and self-honesty necessary to create deeply nourishing and authentic forms of intimacy with others. Once we finally do this, our heart will always guide us through confusion, fear and pain towards relationships that are supportive, vital and joyful.

CHAPTER 27

All Love Is Ultimately Self-Love

A human being is part of a whole, called by us the 'universe' – a part limited in time and space. He experiences himself, his thoughts, and feelings, as something separated from the rest – a kind of optical delusion of his consciousness. This delusion is a kind of prison for us, restricting us to our personal desires and to affection for a few persons nearest us. Our task must be to free ourselves from this prison by widening our circles of compassion to embrace all living creatures and the whole of nature in its beauty.

Albert Einstein

Wherever you are, please take a few slow, deep breaths into your belly. Feel your whole body, from your feet all the way up to the crown of your head, and then down to your fingertips. Please relax any tension you feel and let yourself be. Using each inhalation to open your body and create inner space, welcome everything you're thinking, feeling and experiencing here in this moment. Please be present to your body and your breath.

Initially it seems like a contradiction, but it is true that when we love and help ourselves we are also loving and helping other people, because in reality all of humanity is one interdependent and interconnected web of life. The same is also true for when we give loving support to other people. Anytime we love or help another person, we're once again loving and helping ourselves, because there's no separation between us and anyone or anything that exists. As we learn to love ourselves unconditionally, however, loving anyone or anything 'outside' of ourselves actually becomes a *conscious process* of expanding our own love for ourselves. The important distinction to make here is that once we love ourselves unconditionally, *we actually become capable of sharing love consciously and without conditions*, as opposed to unconsciously 'giving' love to others merely because we feel insecure, inadequate or unlovable, or because we want, need or expect something in return.

Even after all this time, the sun never says to the earth,
'You owe me.' Look what happens with a love like that;
it lights up the whole sky.

Hafiz

From the largest possible perspective, the entire universe can be viewed as one body, or one self, and each of us can be seen as a cell in this universal body. From this perspective, all love is actually self-love, because everyone and everything is a part of this universal self. Another way of understanding this is that the universe is synonymous with God, and in the same way that we're all a part of the universal self, each of us is also a part of God's self. Seen in this light, our own soul, what we perceive to be our individual 'self', is both one with and a unique expression of God, or the universal self. As a single cup full of the ocean, we are not separate from the entire ocean itself.

From this viewpoint, the universe can also be seen as a system that functions solely on love for itself. If you think about the sun's light and energy that nourish life on our planet, we have a perfect example of universal self-love. All life on earth would cease to exist if the sun did not constantly and unconditionally express its love towards our planet. Trees, plants, fruits, vegetables and grains would not grow from the earth. Humans and animals would have nothing to eat. The water we drink would remain frozen and undrinkable. All the trees and plant life would not receive the necessary sunlight and energy to convert carbon dioxide from the atmosphere into the oxygen we all need to breathe. Life on this planet would clearly not exist but for the sun's unconditional love for the aspect of itself that is the earth and all life upon it. The point here is that as much as we perceive ourselves to be separate from the world around us, we can never truly separate ourselves from anyone or anything that exists, regardless of how hard we try.

If you love yourself, you love everybody else as you
do yourself. As long as you love another person less than
yourself, you will not succeed in loving yourself, but if
you love all alike, including yourself, you will love them
as one person and that person is both God and man.
Thus he is the great righteous person who, loving himself,
loves all others equally.

Meister Eckhart

Another great example of self-love in the universe exists between a mother and her child. Most mothers actually love their children far more than they love themselves. In fact, many mothers give of themselves unconditionally to their children, even to their own detriment. Many mothers do this because they inherently know their children's lives are not separate from their own. Most mothers know in their hearts, whether they are conscious of it or not, that once they bring another life into the world, a large part of their purpose is to love and nurture this life unconditionally.

A parent's love for his or her child is one of the most powerful examples of unconditional self-love found in nature. The instinctual drive in both men and women to procreate is the evolutionary impulse of the universe expressing an unconditional love for itself through all forms of life. One of the primary reasons we actually have children is to learn to love ourselves unconditionally. We literally birth aspects of ourselves that we have not learned to love out into the world through our children. This is why our children always mirror back to us the parts of ourselves that we have not fully healed, loved, respected, nurtured, integrated, accepted, forgiven or expressed in our own lives. Fortunately, if you're a parent, through learning to love, respect, accept, appreciate, nurture and forgive your children, you can in turn learn to love and heal all of yourself in the same way.

As children grow and develop they too learn to love, accept, value and be true to themselves, primarily through their relationship with their parents. If you have children, then you're either teaching your children to love themselves through embodying unconditional love yourself, and encouraging them to do the same, or you're unconsciously challenging them and strengthening their love for themselves by not loving them unconditionally. Either way, we all eventually learn the importance of valuing ourselves through this lifelong intimate relationship.

He who experiences the unity of life sees his own Self
in all beings, and all beings in his own Self, and looks
on everything with an impartial eye.

Buddha

Regardless of age, our parents are often the people who influence us the most as we create our lives over time. For this reason, the amount of love we have for ourselves in the present is strongly affected by the amount of love we feel towards our parents. It's difficult to accept ourselves if we cannot learn lovingly to accept our parents as well, ultimately because there is no separation between them and us. For various reasons, this is one of the most challenging tasks we're all called to accomplish, but it is indeed necessary both for the evolution of human consciousness and for mastering an unconditional love for ourselves. Through learning to love, accept, forgive and understand our parents, we also master the lessons necessary to love ourselves and other people. This process reflects the evolutionary force unfolding through our increased expression of love, which is how we as human beings are moving our genetic line forward.

The universe actually expresses itself more fully with each new generation that is born. Through our own genes and our own biological families, God expresses another unique aspect of Itself. This is another significant way that the universe loves itself through each of us. By simply being itself, the universal self – or God – creatively expresses its miraculous intelligence more fully through everyone and everything that comes to be. Through this process, the divine unfolds its greatest creative potential through each of our lives. From this perspective, we are both God and the universe experiencing itself through human life, and as we come to love ourselves unconditionally, we are creating a life that is a unique expression of the universe's love for itself.

CHAPTER 28

The Hidden Key to Being Grateful

There is one simple thing wrong with you – you think you have plenty of time … If you don't think your life is going to last forever, what are you waiting for? Why the hesitation to change? You don't have time for this display, you fool. This, whatever you're doing now, may be your last act on earth. It may very well be your last battle. There is no power which could guarantee that you are going to live one more minute.

Carlos Castaneda, *Journey to Ixtlan*

Wherever you are, please take a few slow, deep breaths into your belly. Feel your whole body, from your feet all the way up to the crown of your head, and then down to your fingertips. Please relax any tension you feel and let yourself be. Using each inhalation to open your body and create inner space, welcome everything you're thinking, feeling and experiencing here in this moment. Please be present to your body and your breath.

Life itself is actually a miracle, and once we value ourselves enough to move beyond fear into a truly authentic life, we experience our existence in a way where this becomes palpable rather than just an idea. The fact that our heart beats, our lungs inhale oxygen, our eyes can read these words, and our cells are carrying out a symphony of functions right now, all of which allow us to feel love, sadness, pleasure and joy in a body, is quite amazing. We only take our life for granted because we get so trapped in fear and the suffering that results. Unintentionally, we live consumed with negative thinking or always striving to be more, do more or have more, which basically causes us to miss our lives in the here and now. Especially in today's fast-paced world, the majority of us are so distracted and stressed that we never make space or take time to just be and enjoy the simple things that make life truly worth living.

Personally I have discovered that there is one master key to feeling genuinely grateful for our lives. This one truth seems to be overlooked in many explorations on how to truly appreciate each day, and I think the reason for this is that it is the most challenging issue to address. Undoubtedly, there is tremendous value in developing habits and practices to acknowledge all the positive things about our life. And it is important to train our mind to appreciate all the blessings we have, even when we're struggling. However, I have found that if we're currently holding back from speaking or acting based on our true feelings in any situation, these fears and the resulting self-rejection stop us from experiencing organic gratitude for simply being alive. In other words, when we're not following our heart, speaking our truth and living authentically both personally and professionally, we're hurting ourselves and preventing ourselves from enjoying life today in the ways we know are possible.

In my experience, deep gratitude is like true intimate love in many respects. It cannot be forced or manufactured. Rather, it must arise naturally and passionately within our being. Yes, over time we can learn to love and appreciate someone in the same way we can develop habits to look for things to be grateful for each morning, evening or throughout the day. However, there is a stronger and purer form of gratitude that we all crave, which I think we all know exists and which only surfaces when our spirit feels free, our heart is open and we feel completely present. This is symbolic of being in love with our life experience more than being burdened by it.

The only way to feel real gratitude on a daily basis is to live in a way in which we value, care for and are true towards ourselves so that we move through the day in ways that make us feel good, alive and well. If we allow guilt, fear or obligation to guide our thoughts, words and actions, then of course life is not going to feel good enough to be thankful for it. Rather, it will continue to feel like a problem or struggle, because we keep making our true feelings, needs and desires wrong in order to keep the peace or to remain comfortable. If we keep rejecting what we feel in our relationships, at home or at work, then life will remain hard. Likewise, if we have unresolved emotional memory stored in our body from challenging chapters in our life, this unprocessed experience will also hold us back from enjoying our lives today.

> Gratefulness for what is there is one of the most powerful tools for creating what is not yet there. What does gratefulness mean? It means you appreciate what is. You value, you give attention to, you honour whatever is here at this moment.

> **Eckhart Tolle**

As we work on being true to ourselves daily and develop the habits that support us to feel alive and well, it is helpful to look intentionally for positive aspects in our experience. Doing so daily opens us to possibilities and opportunities that we unknowingly repel when we're stuck in a contracted or negative mindset. Even when we're not feeling stuck or negative, it's so easy to get caught up in our routines that we rarely take the time to reflect on what is working in our lives, which again closes us off to the nourishing experiences that lead to deep peace and fulfilment. But once again, it's important to keep in mind that we can be perfect in our discipline of looking for things to be grateful for each day, yet if we are betraying ourselves and thus becoming the victim of our fears, we will never find the pure gratitude that only surfaces when we're not settling for less than we're capable of.

Appreciating our health, home, food, clean water, the warmth of the sun's rays, any amount of money or financial support we have, our past education, our teachers, our methods of transportation, our job, our family, our parents, our children, our partner or spouse, our friends, our pets and the intelligent functions of our body, are all blessings that are healthy to value more each day, and which truly help us feel more positive in general. If you stop right now, wherever you are, take a few slow, deep breaths into your belly, feel into your body, into the life that you are, and then look around with openness, can you see, even slightly, the beauty, magic and profundity of this life? If you really look at the trees, the birds, the sky or the people around you, can you feel how life might be a miracle?

If we want to be happy we have to teach ourselves to look for the purpose in our suffering, which is always present and always leads to gratitude for the challenge. If we're living a lie, betraying ourselves or constantly trying to please other people, each day will continue to feel like a struggle and it will remain genuinely hard to feel grateful for our life. At some point it will become crystal clear that being true to ourselves now, even if we are scared or doubtful, is the ultimate lesson and one true path to thanksgiving. Logically, it is quite hard to feel grateful for our life while also fighting our true feelings, needs and desires.

A great deal of the chaos in the world occurs because people don't appreciate themselves.

Chögyam Trungpa Rinpoche

As we learn to value our feelings, needs and desires daily, we develop a natural gratitude for life. Organically, we start to experience each day in deeper and more meaningful ways, because when we do not place conditions on accepting what we feel, we also stop trying to get somewhere else or pretending to be someone other than our true self. When we cease saying I will love myself, be authentic or be happy if I meet a condition in the future, we also stop limiting our openness to how much is already present to enjoy now. In the same way that we learn to feel good about ourselves independently of external circumstances, we also come to accept and appreciate each moment for the purposeful lesson or experience it offers. This process is synonymous with learning to be more present in our lives, with our heart open and vulnerable, as opposed to remaining trapped in our head always thinking about the future. As we learn to be true to ourselves in each situation, we naturally stop feeling we must always be, do or have more to be happy. The direct result of this is an availability to enjoying life in this moment, which is the only place we can receive nourishment from our experiences. Our desperate striving to get somewhere else, to get away from where we are, or to avoid our true feelings is what keeps us chasing our tails and feeling unsatisfied.

For example, you'll be surprised to notice how often you do not actually taste, smell or enjoy the food you're eating or the fluid you're drinking, simply because you're thinking about something you have to do or something that might happen in the future. I'm sure you're aware of restless feelings or of constantly thinking about the next task or short-term pleasure, which typically is a never-ending cycle that's destructive and exhausting emotionally, physically and financially. Thankfully, all we really need to do is be honest daily and focus on what makes us feel alive and well, because this awakens our senses to fully enjoy simple activities like eating, breathing, walking, showering, looking at a flower, gazing at the stars, kissing someone we love or having a real conversation with another miraculous human being. When we're doing what we love and feel in harmony with life, we're spontaneously overcome with pure gratitude throughout the day. Rather than taking our life or the people we love for granted, we can follow our heart, slow down and remain authentic, even when it's uncomfortable to do so and, as a result, not allow our life to pass us by unappreciated.

Practical Questions

If you are one hundred per cent honest with yourself, and fear did not exist, what feelings, needs or desires would you act upon today, which would then lead to natural gratitude?

If you were completely true to yourself today, what would you say and what would you do?

Who and what are you grateful for in your life right now?

What are all of the little things that you can appreciate in and about your life? (*Contemplating these blessings each morning before you get out of bed and every night before you fall asleep is very helpful.*)

Who and what are you grateful for from the past?

What lessons are you grateful for?

Key Affirmations

Thank you for my life. I am so blessed.

Thank you for my body, mind and heart.

Pretending to be happy is not healthy.

Lying to myself to avoid the truth always results in dissatisfaction.

Thank you for my healthy organs, bones and cells.

Thank you for my family and friends.

Thank you for my mother and father.

Thank you for my partner.

Thank you for my personal space and time for myself.

Thank you for my children.

Thank you for the roof over my head.

Thank you for my bed.

Thank you for my job.

Thank you for nourishing food and clean water.

Thank you for the sunshine.

Thank you to the earth.

Thank you for the amazing years to come.

Thank you for today. Thank you for this moment.

CHAPTER 29

Focus on Feeling Alive and Well

Things are coming into your experience in response to your vibration. Your vibration is offered because of the thoughts you are thinking, and you can tell by the way you feel what kinds of thoughts you are thinking. Find good-feeling thoughts, and good-feeling manifestations MUST follow. Make a decision to look for the best feeling aspects of whatever you must give your attention to, and otherwise look only for good-feeling things to give your attention to – and your life will become one of increasingly good-feeling aspects.

Esther and Jerry Hicks,
The Teachings of Abraham

Wherever you are, please take a few slow, deep breaths into your belly. Feel your whole body, from your feet all the way up to the crown of your head, and then down to your fingertips. Please relax any tension you feel and let yourself be. Using each inhalation to open your body and create inner space, welcome everything you're thinking, feeling and experiencing here in this moment. Please be present to your body and your breath.

Each day we are faced with decisions in our personal and professional lives that end up shaping the course of our destiny and the quality of our health, happiness and relationships. If we want to enjoy our life, be well and respect ourselves, it is crucial we each master making choices that are aligned with who we truly are, why we're really here and how we genuinely feel. A simple but powerful way to achieve this is to look at each moment as a fork in the road on the path to our most joyful and authentic life. In any given scenario, at least one direction will always represent a decision that does not feel good in our heart or in our body. In this same situation, at least one other direction or path will eventually reveal itself, which represents a decision that undoubtedly feels good or necessary.

Quite often it can be confusing as to which path is best or healthiest for us to choose. It's very common to feel unclear about which decision feels good and which does not. Rationally we may be able to justify why either choice could be best. In situations like this, it is optimal to wait, or not to make any major choices until a clear knowing surfaces from deep within us. Although this seems like common sense, many of us struggle on a daily basis to know and act on what feels ideal for us. The primary reason for this is that our thoughts are often at odds with what we feel in our heart, because our mind has become very good at trying to protect our heart from emotional pain. This dynamic leads most of us to feel as though our head and our heart are pointing us in opposite directions, when in reality they are both simply guiding us home to ourselves – to our inner truth – here in the present moment. We've just become very good at protecting ourselves from criticism, rejection and judgement.

Because many of us have become so cut off from what we instinctually feel in our body, we now live trapped in our mind, running in mental circles over-analysing important decisions. Fear and self-doubt tend to be the driving forces, which ultimately stop us from direct intuitive action. Ironically, this mental confusion is merely a symptom that's guiding us deeper into what we *feel* right now, so we can finally heal the internalized emotions that stop our heart and mind from feeling united and in agreement. Another very important point to understand is that our new direction forward, or the next step, will not become clear until we've fully learned the lessons we're meant to master in the current situation. We will often stay in something that does not feel good or healthy until we learn to value ourselves sufficiently only to enter into situations and relationships that support us to feel well and free. In other words, we unconsciously stay in situations that do not feel good until we learn to express fully what we feel and need, and find clarity around what we truly want.

In my experience, a YES-WORTHY direction will always reveal itself when we're truly ready to take the next step rather than just running from challenges. Once we have processed all of the emotions and lessons that are present in the current circumstances, the best path forward will become illuminated by positive feelings and clear thoughts that make us feel so good we cannot deny the direction life is now guiding us to explore. When the timing is right, we can then make a choice based on the truth, which is very different to speaking and acting reactively based on fear or denial of the truth.

While waiting for our next step to become well defined, besides simply asking ourselves what we're feeling right now, the most effective thing we can focus our time and energy on is doing the small *constructive* things in life that make us feel good, alive and well. Whether this is taking short walks, writing, reading, taking a bath, making ourselves something warm to drink, exercising, listening to music, painting, or connecting with genuine people, by concentrating on what makes us feel good in the here and now, we can enjoy our lives in the present more – while we simultaneously distinguish where and with whom we currently do not feel good, or where and with whom we do not value ourselves completely.

What activities, small or large, make you feel good, alive and well?

What activities make you feel happy or bring out joy inside of you?

Which people or environments do you feel great around, simply because you can be yourself, or explore yourself, or do what feels true and healthy for you?

By identifying your answers to these questions and by focusing on these activities and relationships as much as possible each day, you will begin to increase the amount of time you feel good, alive and well overall. With consistency, this process will bring significant clarity to decisions, goals, plans and interactions with others, because the more you focus your energy on simply feeling good, the more you will naturally feel and know which choices are most aligned with who you really are, why you're really here, and the quality of life you'd like to create.

Because the purpose of human life is to enjoy it fully, while learning what it means to love unconditionally, filling our days with the small things that make us feel great is vital to creating a fulfilling life. The small daily choices that build our energy, mood and health, as opposed to those that drain our energy or bring us down, are what provide us with the fuel we need to make our larger visions, goals and desires our lived reality. Without focusing on the small things that make us feel good daily, we cannot access the energy we need to move forward and create a life that supports our happiness and life purpose. Regardless of how attractive a certain lifestyle, career, relationship or dream-reality is, we will never create it without acting in ways that make us feel better and better each day. For this reason, every single moment offers a junction on our path to enjoying life daily. YES-WORTHY opportunities always present themselves to us, especially when we're focused on what makes us feel well. If we can learn to act when it feels good, but wait to act when it does not, even when we feel insecure, anxious or scared, our heart will always guide us towards the lasting love, joy and peace we're seeking.

CHAPTER 30

Inner Wealth and Financial Freedom

Let us more and more insist on raising funds of love, of kindness, of understanding, of peace. Money will come if we seek first the Kingdom of God – the rest will be given.

Mother Teresa

Wherever you are, please take a few slow, deep breaths into your belly. Feel your whole body, from your feet all the way up to the crown of your head, and then down to your fingertips. Please relax any tension you feel and let yourself be. Using each inhalation to open your body and create inner space, welcome everything you're thinking, feeling and experiencing here in this moment. Please be present to your body and your breath.

We all hold different beliefs about what constitutes true wealth and success. However, anyone who has chased after money, material wealth or worldly success as a top priority at the expense of their health, their relationships or their inner states of peace and happiness deeply knows that true wealth and success are not measured by the amount of money we have in the bank or by the material possessions we own. In today's world, many of us have been raised to think of success primarily in terms of attaining financial wealth and material abundance, but, again, these achievements mean nothing if we do not have love for ourselves, love for our lives and love for the people in our lives. If we're not at peace and happy within ourselves, our relationships and our careers, even if we have both fame and fortune, just how wealthy and successful are we, really?

Inevitably, there always comes a time when we realize that true wealth comes when we have love in our heart, love in our relationships and love for our work. When we're at peace, healthy, happy and fulfilled, we've cultivated a type of inner success that nothing and no one can ever take away – a form of lived prosperity that nothing could ever truly compare to. Deep down we all want to live each day feeling that our lives express our innermost truths and values, because we know this is the only way to respect ourselves. We all want to wake up each morning with clarity about who we are and passion for why we are here, because we know that finding this treasure-house unlocks a type of courage, confidence and integrity that no amount of money could ever create or buy.

For what is a man profited, if he shall gain the whole world, and lose his own soul?

Matthew 16:26

For those who are struggling to create financial freedom it is crucial to understand that it is the depth of our inner wealth and success that determines the degree to which we create a lasting and fulfilling relationship to wealth in the outer world. As much as we've all been led to believe otherwise, accumulating material wealth or financial security without attending to our inner peace, happiness and life calling will only result in dissatisfaction. Even though we tend to think that money and worldly success are the key ingredients in living a happy and satisfying life, on a deeper level we all know that these things will never satiate our hunger for clarity of purpose, heart-to-heart connection and true self-respect. As odd as it may seem at first, learning how to love and value ourselves is not only the key to transforming our suffering and fulfilling our life's purpose, but it is also a very effective way to create sustainable financial freedom as well.

For those of us who have already created financial freedom, but are now looking for true love, peace, health, happiness or deeper meaning, the previous chapters in this book offer you the keys to creating a type of wealth that no amount of money or external achievement could ever purchase. Considering this, if you've already created financial wealth in your life, it is empowering to ask yourself: *why? Where did your motivations come from? Were you conditioned to make money by your family and society? Were you seeking love, approval, attention or praise? Were you afraid for your survival or the survival of your family? Did you accumulate material wealth out of what you believed was necessity? Did you believe that money and material wealth would make you more lovable, attractive, emotionally secure or happy? Did you believe money would give you power, influence or control?*

If we have struggled with money, or have witnessed unhealthy relationships to money, or view money as evil, then it is easy to become trapped by the idea that one must renounce money or reject the material world in order to find lasting peace, happiness or fulfilment. However, if we stop to consider that everything in the universe is unquestionably a part of God, it becomes clear that there's no true separation between our concepts of what is 'spiritual' and what is 'material'. When we reject the material world, for any reason, we're actually denying a very large part of our physical experience that we must eventually embrace. It's important to remember that money and material possessions will never make us more lovable, more worthy, more deserving, happier, more connected or more emotionally secure. Yet, at the same time, if we truly want freedom from our suffering, we eventually have to respect both the inner and the outer aspects of our lives. Although many people close their heart and mind to making money or creating material wealth, money itself is not bad in any way. *It is our relationship to money that is either healthy or not.* In fact, money is just another form of atomic energy or love. If our happiness and sense of self-worth are based on how much money or material wealth we have, then our relationship to money is both unhealthy and limiting. However, if we know that money cannot buy happiness or love, and that we must be true to ourselves and answer our inner calling as a top priority, then our relationship to money can be both healthy and liberating.

The same logic also applies to the material world of 'things'. Things are not bad in and of themselves. There is nothing wrong or sinful about enjoying beautiful material objects. Just like money, it is our inner relationship to these material objects (or lack thereof) that is either healthy or unhealthy. If we believe that material possessions will make us more lovable, worthy, happy or less insecure, then our relationship to the 'things' we either have or desire is definitely unhealthy. Likewise, if we identify with our material possessions and thus believe they somehow define us or make us superior or inferior to others in any way, then again our relationship to these material objects will always cause us to suffer.

When we learn to prioritize our inner wealth – our peace, health, happiness and love for ourselves – we can enjoy the physical world without being attached to anything. If we know that 'things' will never bring us happiness, deep meaning or true love, we can both create and experience all forms of material wealth without losing ourselves to them or deluding ourselves into thinking we will ever find what we're really looking for outside ourselves.

> *To live content with small means; to seek elegance*
> *rather than luxury, and refinement rather than fashion;*
> *to be worthy, not respectable, and wealthy, not, rich;*
> *to listen to stars and birds, babes and sages, with an*
> *open heart; to study hard; to think quietly, act frankly,*
> *talk gently, await occasions, hurry never; in a word,*
> *to let the spiritual, unbidden and unconscious, grow*
> *up through the common. This is my symphony.*
>
> **William Ellery Channing**

Whether you'd like to create greater financial freedom or you'd simply like to find a more fulfilling approach to making money, you're being called to open your mind and accept a new way of thinking about money and, in particular, its direct relationship to love. Practically speaking, I've found it crucial to understand the intimate relationship between (1) how much we love ourselves, (2) how much love we give to others, (3) how open and vulnerable our heart is, and (4) how wealthy and successful we are externally. In other words, if we truly want to thrive in today's evolving world, we have to master the intimate dynamic that's always unfolding between money, love and the energetic nature of our universe.

Science has shown how everything in the universe is made of one fundamental energetic substance, which we call *atoms* and which also drive the function and movement of all life and matter in its various forms. Practically speaking, both love and money can be viewed simply as different manifestations of the same basic atomic energy that makes up everything that exists. Beneath the apparent differences between our body, our thoughts, money, material objects and the state of being we call love, there is one underlying, uniting force or tapestry – which is the intelligent, logical, aware and energetic universe.

At this stage you might be wondering: *why is this important to understand in terms of living a wealthy, successful and financially liberated life?*

The reason these insights are so important is that while there are many ways to make money and create material wealth in the short term, *there is only one way to manifest sustainable, long-term financial freedom and live a fulfilling life that is aligned with the universe, our life's purpose, our passion, and with who we truly are.* This one way is always through following our heart and through living openly and vulnerably. Even though you might be sceptical at first, the truth remains that it's only through continuously expanding our heart's capacity to give and receive love that we can open ourselves to the unlimited stream of universal wealth-love-energy that is always available to us.

Practically speaking, we create our lives with the subtle energies of our beliefs, thoughts, emotions, actions and spoken words. If we explore this process of creation on a deeper level, we'll naturally see that our beliefs, thoughts and emotions ultimately drive the actions we take and the words we speak. From this perspective, it becomes clear that the more consistently our beliefs, thoughts and emotions come from a place of kindness, acceptance and honesty – or in other words, from a place of unconditional self-love and passion for life – the more our actions and spoken words will come from an energy of love and passion as well. It logically follows that the more our beliefs, thoughts, emotions, actions and spoken words are grounded in a loving and purpose driven energy, then the more our lives in the outer world will reflect back to us this inner health, kindness and positivity.

When we truly value and respect ourselves, as opposed to solely chasing money out of fear, insecurity and inadequacy, we create positive situations both personally and professionally, because this is the natural by-product of a healthy relationship to ourselves where we focus on what we love each day. In being true to ourselves, we become happier about the work we do and the life we live. When we actually give ourselves permission to find our craft and calling, and commit to mastering it, the amount of energy and love we have for every single situation becomes extremely strong, magnetic and expansive. This is why people who are truly happy, inspired and genuine always attract amazing people and opportunities. It doesn't matter what form of passionate living and sharing we engage in; all that matters is that we find work or a way of living that is personally meaningful and enjoyable. Then, as long as we're taking care of our health and doing what we love each day, we always receive back the energy we give out in the forms we need most at any particular point in our lives. Whether it's money, food, shelter, work, emotional support or companionship, we receive what we genuinely need when we're committed to being authentic and happy over and above living in fear, maintaining pride or trying to avoid judgement. If we wake up each morning and give our heart fully to what we're doing, we'll always have sufficient wealth in the outer world. This is the case because the more we love ourselves, the more we're able to love other people and life in general. And the more we're able to love ourselves, others and daily life, the more open and vulnerable our heart becomes. The more open and vulnerable our heart becomes, the more we're able to give and receive love in its various forms (i.e. money, compassion, presence, energy, inspiration, etc.). So, as mind-boggling as it may seem, the amount of money and material wealth we attract, sustain and enjoy is directly proportional to how open our heart is and how much love we're willing to give to ourselves and to the world. Even though our relationships to money and material survival tend to be quite complicated, confusing and stressful, creating meaningful financial freedom becomes simpler once we understand how the amount of energy and love we receive back from life is equal to how fully we've answered our life's true calling.

> *For true love is inexhaustible; the more you give, the more*
> *you have. And if you go to draw at the true fountainhead,*
> *the more water you draw, the more abundant is its flow.*
> **Antoine de Saint-Exupéry**

Although you may not hear this often enough, you are completely capable of creating the financial freedom you desire. Whether or not you experience this freedom all depends on how much responsibility you're willing to take for the amount of love, acceptance, value and respect you cultivate for yourself and your life purpose. Our individual capacity to create financial freedom is unlimited – if this is what you desire. Most of us don't actually need that much money to be happy though. We just need enough to take care of our responsibilities while we spend time with those we love and enjoy our lives as much as possible each day. Deep down we all know that money can't buy the most valuable things in life. So even if we had all the money in the world, we still could not purchase the heart-to-heart connection, self-respect, peace, happiness or love we're seeking.

When we follow our heart and go after what we're sincerely called to do, we'll always create exactly what we need to support our lifestyle and way of being in the world. I have found that when we're focused on fulfilling our soul's purpose, the universe and God always provide us with everything we need to enjoy our lives and live with peace in our heart. It is ultimately a waste of time and energy to judge another person based on how much money they make or what they have. All we can do is focus on being true to ourselves so that we create what we personally desire and feel good about.

Although we're not taught to think this way, we do live in an infinite universe, so there's always enough energy, money and love to go around. The mere fact that one person has a large amount of something does not mean there's not enough for us to fulfil our own unique potential and live each day to the fullest. Life merely asks each of us to be patient, persistent and kind towards ourselves as we cultivate the inner wealth and self-worth that always precede the external wealth and long-term success that has real lasting value. Since we're not only one hundred per cent responsible for what we create, but also one hundred per cent capable of creating anything we really need, it's entirely up to us to break through the inner blocks that are stopping us from opening our heart, appreciating the miracle of our life, and giving ourselves permission to be happy. In the end, there are no words to describe the high-quality prosperity and aliveness that are born from being true to ourselves and living passionately with each word and action.

Practical Questions

What do wealth and success mean to you?

What will your life look like when you feel wealthy and successful?

If you had all the money you desired right now, what would you go do, create or experience?

Do you actually need more money to do, create and experience *all* of these things?

Do you feel that your heart is open? Do you feel that you love life and people with your whole heart? If not, why not? When will you take the risk and give all of yourself to your life and your purpose?

Are you professionally engaged in work that you love?

If not, when will you stop compromising yourself?

Do you overspend or compulsively spend money? *If so, can you see that the reason you do this is because you're still not accepting yourself fully? Can you see how spending money numbs you temporarily to certain things within yourself and your life? Can you see how underneath this habit there are things about you, your life and your past that you still do not love, accept, forgive or feel good about? Can you see how the root cause of your overspending is connected to where in your life you're compromising, abandoning, betraying and thus hurting yourself? Can you see that regardless of what you buy, your insecurities do not go away? Can you see how subconsciously you believe having more or buying more, will make you more lovable, more attractive or more secure in yourself? Can you see how this is connected to the conditional love, acceptance and approval you seek from others? Lastly, can you see how you might be happier with yourself if you were to focus more of your time and energy on meaningful projects and activities that are driven by your life purpose, passion and calling?*

Are you afraid of spending money? *If so, can you see how you might feel you are not worthy or valuable enough to invest in? Can you see that you fear feeling the insecurity and inadequacy within you and thus try to cover them by hoarding money or material possessions? Are you aware of your fears around giving and receiving love? Can you see how you might fear being rejected, abandoned, betrayed, used or hurt, and thus feel the need to hold back and over-control yourself and your true desires? Can you see how underneath your fear of 'not having enough', you're really afraid of accepting and expressing what you truly feel, want and need for yourself? Can you also see that you do not have complete trust in life because you do not trust yourself? Lastly, again, can you see how you might feel freer to give in all ways if you were focused more on projects and activities that are driven by your life purpose, passion and calling? Can you see how by taking this approach to money and life, you could regularly generate income and receive what you need to sustain a meaningful, generous and inspired way of life?*

Key Affirmations

Self-love and self-respect are my path to true wealth
and success.

Money will never buy me true love or happiness.

No amount of money can make me more lovable than
I already am.

I deserve true love just as I am.

I deserve the financial freedom to live a joyful life that I love.

I have everything I need to create a wealthy, successful
and fulfilling life.

Loving myself is the path to financial fulfilment and freedom.

The more I love myself, the more wealthy and
successful I am.

My health and happiness are more valuable than money.

To know my worth and value, I have to express my true feelings
and follow my heart.

Money and love are energy. The more love I have for myself,
the more wealth I will create.

Life supports me in all ways when I am true to myself and
my purpose.

CHAPTER 31

Take the Vulnerable Path

It is not the critic who counts; not the man who points out how the strong man stumbles, or where the doer of deeds could have done them better. The credit belongs to the man who is actually in the arena, whose face is marred by dust and sweat and blood; who strives valiantly; who errs, who comes short again and again, because there is no effort without error and shortcoming; but who does actually strive to do the deeds; who knows great enthusiasms, the great devotions; who spends himself in a worthy cause; who at the best knows in the end the triumph of high achievement, and who at the worst, if he fails, at least fails while daring greatly, so that his place shall never be with those cold and timid souls who neither know victory nor defeat.

Theodore Roosevelt

Wherever you are, please take a few slow, deep breaths into your belly. Feel your whole body, from your feet all the way up to the crown of your head, and then down to your fingertips. Please relax any tension you feel and let yourself be. Using each inhalation to open your body and create inner space, welcome everything you're thinking, feeling and experiencing here in this moment. Please be present to your body and your breath.

One of the most important realizations I've ever had in my life is that it is not until we jump, take a leap of faith and risk everything we've known before that life can give us what we desire most. The logic behind this is that when we allow ourselves to be the victim of our fears – meaning we allow our fears of failure, judgement, pain, rejection or the unknown to stop us from being true to ourselves or from pursuing what feels good to us – our heart remains closed, which literally blocks us from receiving the very things we've been seeking or asking for. It's like being tortured and starved of food for weeks, but when someone opens our cage and offers us nourishing food, we are scared to leave the cage and we keep our hands over our mouth, refusing to receive the very things we need. In other words, when we allow our fears to drive our choices, the actions *we do not take* and the *opportunities we allow to pass us by* are symbolic of us rejecting both ourselves and the life we were born to live.

Conversely, when we find the courage to face our fears directly, to go after what we dream of, and thus step into the unknown, our heart literally opens, which then renders us ready to receive finally what we've been longing to feel, achieve and experience. Once we're completely exhausted from fighting and rejecting our true feelings, it is time for us to take the risk, to step out beyond the cold comfort we know we're not satisfied with, and to embrace the high-quality life that's waiting beyond our self-destructive attempt to control everything. It is time to admit the truth to ourselves, to express it kindly and authentically, and to trust that whatever dies or changes in the process of becoming fully ourselves is meant to be and in everyone's best interest.

Leap and the net will appear.

John Burroughs

Authentic long-term success, whether it's in life, love, business, health or spiritual awareness, is the direct result of our commitment to remain openhearted and vulnerable. In my experience, all successful endeavours – whether the goal is to love myself unconditionally, to fulfil my life's purpose, to build a thriving business, to express my attraction to a woman, to create a healthy relationship, or to find inner peace – boil down to my willingness to overcome rejection and the fear of being rejected. In other words, I have found that it is a persistent willingness to jump, to push the edge of my comfort zone, to wear my heart on my sleeve, to express the truth in my heart, and to continually follow what feels good and healthy – no matter what – that opens the door to truly enjoying life.

Through courageously facing both rejection and the fear of rejection we eventually learn not to fear them, because the self-respect and self-confidence that come from being true to ourselves – from not holding ourselves back – is more valuable than a false sense of pride or security. At some point it becomes apparent that the pain we create by rejecting ourselves is far greater and far more destructive than any pain we could ever experience from being rejected or criticized by someone else for any reason. Once we finally understand this high truth, both the possibility of rejection and the fear of rejection lose their power over us, which then enables us to live vulnerably and to jump bravely whenever life calls us into the new or the unknown.

Practical Questions

If you knew that you would die one year from today, what would you focus your time and energy on? What would you go and do, see and experience? Who would you call or reconnect with? Who would you forgive? Who would you spend more quality time with?

What does your most liberated and joyful life look like? What do you imagine the life of your dreams to feel like?

What steps do you know you need to take in order to make your larger vision and dream your reality? Why are you avoiding these steps? When will you stop making excuses and finally go after what you believe in, value, want and love?

Where in your life are you settling for less than you know you are capable of?

Where and with whom in your life are you still compromising yourself and denying your greatness?

Once again, are you waiting for your children to age, your parents to die or your intimate relationship to end before you start living your life the way you want to? If so, why?

When is enough truly enough? When will you say enough settling, enough compromising, enough sickness, enough misery and enough living in fear?

If not now, then when? If not today, then when?

Key Affirmations

I was not born to suffer. I was born to live my life to the fullest.

I deserve the best in every aspect of my life.

I deserve to be happy.

It's never too late to start over. I can re-create anything I need to.

I am always supported and protected.

I will not settle for less than I am worthy, deserving or capable of.

I have everything I need within me to create a fulfilling life
that I love.

CHAPTER 32

The Final Question

There are only two mistakes one can make along the road to truth; not going all the way, and not starting.

Buddha

After years of desperately searching for happiness, purpose and true love, I started to ask myself: *If the most liberating perspective is to view ourselves as God in human form, which implies we both chose and created our lives and experiences in their entirety, then why would we ever choose to suffer or create pain for ourselves or others? Theologically, this question can be framed as: why did God create suffering? If we are that intelligent and powerful, why would we ever choose to hurt ourselves by not loving ourselves? Why would we ever choose to forget who we truly are or why we came here? Why would we create an ego, or a separate self, and thereby forget our unity with God, the universe and all life? Why would we choose to forget that our true nature is an infinite source of pure unconditional love and that we do not need to search for love outside of ourselves?*

I asked myself these questions regularly for a period of time, because they felt like the final piece of the puzzle in my quest for lasting inner peace and freedom. I felt that because you and I are one with God, we should be able to understand the mind and logic of God. Eventually, you could say I was shown, or that I remembered, that the reason why we all choose to create suffering for ourselves is that we may bring unconditional love, kindness and forgiveness into the physical world. We also choose to experience what does not feel good in order to create a contrast with what does feel good, which then provides a touchstone to direct our choices and actions towards whatever supports our health and happiness.

The logic behind this ultimate spiritual truth is that if we can view our suffering as a purposeful choice that we made in order, eventually, to learn to forgive ourselves for the act of making this choice, starting with our choice in parents and all the challenges that came with it, we can truly take responsibility for our healing and happiness at the very core of our psyche and being. If we are indeed God in human form, then we created this process specifically to bring forth our capacity to accept and forgive others, which is the essence of unconditional love. In knowing what it's like to feel pain, having hurt both ourselves and others in the past, we cannot help but be more kind, forgiving and compassionate. We also learn not to take things so personally, which is liberating in and of itself. The reason this awareness is so important is that if we truly want to enjoy our lives, find fulfilling work and create healthy relationships, we have no choice but to take full responsibility for *everything that we experience*. This means we cannot blame God, our parents, our children, our spouse or anyone for any reason, because when we do, we continue to create suffering, depression and disease.

In the beginning of my own healing and spiritual journey I believed that responsibility and freedom could not exist together. However, I later realized that in order to liberate myself from suffering and truly enjoy my life, I had to commit fully to my life's purpose and to relating to myself with loving acceptance every day. I had to take complete responsibility for every single thought, emotion, spoken word, action and experience in my life. Today, it's only through a devotion to being kind and true to myself in each situation, even when I'm scared, that life continually opens doors to an ever-expanding freedom, joy and peace. I am humbled each day as I accept my life challenges as though they were agreements I made with the universe and with God before this lifetime, because by doing so, I find the strength and courage to walk my destined path to the end, knowing that giving up or turning around are not options and will only lead back to suffering.

CHAPTER 33

Live Fully
Before You Die

The one who follows the crowd will usually get no further than the crowd. The one who walks alone is likely to find himself in places no one has ever been.

Albert Einstein

The fact that you have read this book means you've been called to transform the self-destructive habits and views that have been passed down by your parents, your genetic bloodline and modern society. You are being challenged to break the cycle of self-harm and self-rejection, because it has to stop somewhere.

Many of us have now watched people we love battle with addiction, depression, illness, fear and relationship problems, while simultaneously trying to raise families, put food on the table, or simply find some degree of peace, happiness or connection. The sad but purposeful truth is that most people were never taught how to love themselves unconditionally or why it's so important to master it as early as possible. Like you and I, no one really learns how to be happy and well. The people who influenced us as children could not show us or teach us what they themselves were still struggling to learn. They couldn't help us develop a healthy emotional awareness, let alone help us prevent depression or disease, because they still didn't know how to care for or value themselves very well.

It's easy to see how for generations people all over the world have struggled to live in ways that are joyful, authentic and satisfying. This is why the desire to be free from suffering has always surfaced organically from deep within the human heart. In the end, the desires for peace, purpose, health, happiness and genuine connection always hold the highest value once the dust storms of fear, hatred, vanity and materialism settle and give way to the clarity and light of unconditional love, kindness, honesty and mutual respect.

Regardless of our age or stage in life, when we look back on our own lives and consider the trials we've both endured and survived, it's hard not to feel compassion for ourselves and for the people closest to us. When we're not reactive, hurt, angry or scared, and we really stop to reflect on the challenging lessons life presents to everyone in unique yet equal forms, it's difficult not to feel sympathy for our planet, for our ancestors and for the generations to come. As human beings we all struggle, and yet we still find countless ways to judge ourselves for feeling the way we feel, for creating the lives we have or for being in the situations we're in. However, when we finally find the courage to relate to ourselves with honesty and kindness, we can easily see the truth that we all do our best with what we know, and sometimes we don't know what we don't know until we're forced to learn it, which typically comes about through pain.

> *He who learns must suffer*
> *And even in our sleep pain that cannot forget*
> *Falls drop by drop upon the heart*
> *And in our own despite, against our will,*
> *Comes wisdom to us by the awful grace of God.*
>
> **Aeschylus**

Eventually, I think we'll all remember that love is the prism through which every human need is met. In my opinion, from the very beginning of this universe right through to the beginning of this lifetime, we all take form and are created in the energy of love, which is why, whether we're aware of it or not, it has always been our destiny to return home to the source of love from which we came, only to realize that we never actually left. Our depth of peace is simply an evolution in how clearly we (1) perceive the truth of our existence, and (2), feel the real love that gives it meaning.

We're all born knowing we came here to enjoy our life, our body, and to experience love as completely as possible. We know we did not come into this world to become stuck, numb, unhappy or unwell. Although some of us believe we have to die or be reborn to be free, the truth is that physical death is not the real road to salvation. Our true liberation is waiting for us here and now, in this lifetime and body. All we have to do is find the courage to speak our truth and follow our heart no matter what.

When I personally began to look for freedom from my suffering, someone gave me a plaque that said, 'The journey of a thousand miles begins with one step.' The journey back home to our true self after years of being lost in pleasing others, in the material world, in a family, in a relationship, in a job, in an addiction or in a false image of ourselves is indeed a process. Thankfully, when we're finally prepared to face our struggles honestly, we not only find freedom from them more quickly than we presume, we also prevent further suffering for ourselves.

As I've shared before, in my own quest for inner peace and happiness, I found that underneath my thinking mind and changing emotional state there is infinite space within me – an underlying and unifying stillness – that is so full of love and clarity that no words could ever do justice in describing it. I have no doubt whatsoever that this space inside of me also exists deep within you and every single human being. This place I'm referring to is so full of potential, creative intelligence and vital energy that language does not have words that come close to defining it. I think the most accurate road sign I've ever seen pointing in this direction was when I opened a Chinese fortune cookie and found the following words:

One cloud is enough to eclipse a whole sun.

Thomas Fuller

In light of how much we suffer from a single fear, limiting thought, uncomfortable emotion, painful choice or traumatic experience, it is absolutely amazing how true this statement is.

I am reminded increasingly each day of how fragile and precious life is. Because our consciousness or our energy is both immortal and eternal, we unknowingly feel we're invincible or that we can delay living our life, assuming we will have time later or in the future to follow our heart, pursue our dreams, take better care of ourselves, or be true to ourselves completely. As strong as we are, and even though we've all overcome so much to be where we are today, we can never know when our final day will come. We are never guaranteed a specific number of years in this body. The question then becomes: *How can we live fully before we die? How can we love wholeheartedly before it's too late?*

If we keep living a lie, living in fear, blaming others or holding on to anger, then our life will pass us by and we will die suffering mentally and emotionally, or in physical pain, and full of regret. Or, we can speak our truth and follow our heart today, and in so doing enjoy life and the people we love as much as possible right now. Rather than waiting for a future that may never come, our challenge is to stop hurting ourselves and to give ourselves permission to be honest, happy and well today.

Life seems to take away anything or anyone we do not appreciate, so our calling is respectfully to pay attention to the whispers of our heart in every situation, because this leads to a body that feels good to be in and thus worthy of our loving care. Then, rather than living a life defined by stress, constant thinking, non-stop running and frustration, we can slow down and enjoy each day, each breath, each meal, each bird song, each moment of the sun's warmth, each rainfall, each flower, each friend, each kiss, each hug, and the many other pleasurable aspects of being alive. When our heart is open and we're actually present to our life, we can choose to focus our time and energy hour by hour, day by day, in ways that genuinely make the most of our time here. This is how we actually value our existence.

Personally, expressing my true feelings, focusing on work I am passionate about and allowing myself space to do what feels good for my heart and body each day is how I've finally come to feel 'enough' in myself. Although at times it was very confusing, this is how I came to feel good enough, hard-working enough and worthy enough of love, happiness, respect and being valued. It's how I stopped creating further suffering and put an end to thinking I always had to be, do or have more. It's also how I found a loving appreciation for the miracles we all came here to experience. I've found it very helpful to remain mindful that whatever is unresolved from the past, whether from yesterday, last month or five years ago, blocks us from being fully open to enjoying who or what is in front of us today. That said, my hope for you is that you will stop rejecting yourself, stop betraying yourself and stop making your feelings, needs and desires wrong. You did not come here to suffer in silence, to please other people or to make others happy. Regardless of what others think or say, it's okay to be your true self, to feel as you do, to talk about it, and to live each day in ways that feel good and for which you respect yourself.

Moving forward, may you find the courage, strength and love for yourself to live, speak and act with truth and kindness in every situation. May you be at peace in your heart, healthy, happy and fulfilled. May you be free from your suffering and its causes today and always.

Sincerely and warmly,

Blake D Bauer

Acknowledgements

I would like to thank the team at Watkins Publishing. I am very grateful for your support in bringing this book to a larger number of people internationally who are genuinely seeking help. I am grateful to Michael Mann, Jo Lal and Etan Ilfeld for trusting in my work. I am also grateful to Nick Fawcett for helping me strengthen the manuscript. I would like to thank Slav Todorov for overseeing this new edition and also Francesca Corsini for designing the new front cover. Your efforts will help the book reach even more people around the world.

I would like to thank my agent Susan Mears for your commitment, persistence and guidance. I would also like to thank my publicist Gail Torr for helping me share my work and ensuring it reaches those who might benefit from it.

I would like to thank Robert Mueller for designing the cover for the previous edition of this book. Your amazing skill helped this message reach, and thus empower, countless people. Thank you so very much.

I would also like to thank my mother and father, Abbe and Marshall, for your support over the years. Without you I would not have been able to walk my destined path to the degree I have. I would like to thank Maxine for your support and for teaching me so much. Your presence, strength and friendship have been blessings indescribable by words. To my beautiful sister Cassandra, thank you for your unconditional love and encouragement. You continue to be the most amazing friend and inspiration. Thank you for choosing me to be your brother. I would not want to live this life without you. To my late brother Jason, thank you for challenging me over the years and for helping me to open my mind to realities I did not know existed. I am eternally grateful that we were brothers in this lifetime. Love is Law. Life is Love. To my late grandmother, Sophie, thank you for your unconditional love, care and concern. Who knows where our entire family would be today had we not had you in our lives. To the rest of my family, both genetic and soul-based, thank you for being in my life and for teaching me so many lessons about what truly matters.

To my ancestors, both biological and spiritual, thank you for paving the way and preparing the soil for me to remember what I had forgotten. To all of my teachers over the years, thank you for showing up. To all of my beautiful clients past, present and future, thank you for entrusting me with the honour of witnessing and supporting you in your healing and awakening. I am eternally grateful. You humble me and you make my life largely worth living. From the bottom of my heart, thank you. Last but not least, to you the reader, thank you for sharing your journey with me. It is an honour.

About Blake D Bauer

Blake D Bauer is an internationally sought-after speaker, teacher and consultant with an extensive background in psychology, alternative medicine, nutrition, traditional healing and mindfulness meditation. He is considered by many to be a modern meditation and qi gong master. Based on both his personal experience overcoming deep suffering, addiction and adversity, as well as his professional success with thousands of people worldwide, his pioneering work integrates what he's found to be the most effective approaches to mental, emotional and physical health.

You can learn more about Blake D Bauer at www.unconditional-selflove.com.

Notes

Notes

WATKINS

Sharing Wisdom Since
1893

The story of Watkins dates back to 1893, when the scholar of esotericism John Watkins founded a bookshop, inspired by the lament of his friend and teacher Madame Blavatsky that there was nowhere in London to buy books on mysticism, occultism or metaphysics. That moment marked the birth of Watkins, soon to become the home of many of the leading lights of spiritual literature, including Carl Jung, Rudolf Steiner, Alice Bailey and Chögyam Trungpa.

Today, the passion at Watkins Publishing for vigorous questioning is still resolute. Our wide-ranging and stimulating list reflects the development of spiritual thinking and new science over the past 120 years. We remain at the cutting edge, committed to publishing books that change lives.

DISCOVER MORE . . .

Read our blog

Watch and listen to
our authors in action

Sign up to
our mailing list

JOIN IN THE CONVERSATION

 WatkinsPublishing   @watkinswisdom

 watkinsbooks    watkinswisdom    watkins-media

Our books celebrate conscious, passionate, wise and happy living.
Be part of the community by visiting

www.watkinspublishing.com